# Contents

KT-378-691

# CONTAINER
# GARDENING
■ All Year Round ■

## Yvonne Rees & David Palliser

First published in 1990 by
The Crowood Press Ltd
Gipsy Lane, Swindon
Wiltshire SN2 6DQ

This impression 1990

© The Crowood Press Ltd 1990

**British Library Cataloguing in Publication Data**

Rees, Yvonne
   Container gardening.
   1. Gardens. Plants. Cultivation in containers
   I. Title   II. Palliser, David
   635'.048

ISBN 1 85223 303 6

Grateful thanks to Joan Clifton at Clifton Nurseries for her advice on container
plants and kind co-operation with much of the photography.

**Picture Credits**

All colour photographs by Steve Wooster except those by the following, to
whom thanks are due: Dave Pike for Figs 60, 64, 70, 76, 79, 84, 85, 93, 94, 100,
101, 102, 103, 104, 105, 106, 107, 108, 109, 110, 111, 112, 113, 116, 117, 118,
and 119; Rokes Ltd for Figs 6 and 47; Photos Horticultural for Fig 9; Spanish
Art and Ceramics for Figs 22, 31 (a)–(d), and 37; Chilstone Garden Ornaments
for Figs 5, 8, 15, and 16; Briastone/R.S. Trippier for the title page, Figs 11 and
12; Unwins Seeds Ltd for Figs 55, 65, 89, and 114; and Suttons Seeds Ltd for
Figs 54, 66, and 115.
All colour artwork by Claire Upsdale-Jones.

Typeset by Chippendale Type, Otley, West Yorkshire.
Printed and bound by Times Publishing Group, Singapore.

# Preface

Our first flat was a Victorian basement with large, wide, stone windowsills perfect for pots and troughs of plants. We not only grew flowers to brighten up the view, but also experimented with fruit and vegetables – dwarf green beans, tiny cherry tomatoes and strawberries – to which the postman helped himself as soon as they ripened. On either side of the front door we managed to get two sunflowers in big pots to grow to nearly seven feet before they keeled over in the wind.

Since then, our container ideas have expanded into a mobile herb garden which moves with us from house to house; freestanding pot-grown climbers trained up wired shapes; and a tub-planted miniature orchard and fruit garden. We have seen a tremendous growth of interest in the kinds of plants suitable for growing in pots and tubs, a far better range of containers, and the development of dwarfed, compact and trailing plants to meet the new demand, especially in towns and cities where inhabitants are eager for outdoor space and exploit every possible area from roof to balcony, backyard and basement.

Everyone seems to be creating indoor/ outdoor living areas complete with stylish furniture, sophisticated barbecue cooking facilities, smart paved, tiled or timber floors, often matching the floors indoors, accessories, and – oh yes, plants! Plants have become a design tool. They must also be smart and stylish; exactly the right shade, dramatically shaped and arranged in perfectly balanced displays that blend and contrast all their best features, while looking completely natural. This has led to a greater awareness of the more interesting foliage plants, the use of trees and shrubs in containers, as well as spring bulbs and summer annuals. Experiments with striking evergreens and other low maintenance species, combined with the easy-care and instantaneous nature of gardening in pots and tubs, understandably appeals strongly to today's gardeners with their busy lifestyles.

Confining plants in decorative containers has also kindled the interest of those with large gardens. Sizeable plots are being divided into garden 'rooms', creating small seating and patio

*Fig 1   A sheltered balcony or roof garden can become a leafy haven with a careful arrangement of container plants.*

5

*Fig 3   Try to achieve groups of different heights and designs rather than mixing materials.*

*Fig 2   Brighten up a dull entrance with a profusion of summer flowers.*

areas within the main scheme and using urns and pots as focal points or to soften any sharp edges; round the pool, on walls and balconies, in the centre of a formal garden, on either side of a garden seat, ranged along steps, or simply filling in an otherwise bare or boring area with seasonal interest. There has been a revival of interest in the old techniques of pruning and training fruit trees into compact and decorative shapes, in topiary for shaping small-leaved evergreens into geometrical designs, and in devising

standard and half standard trees for ornamental tub display.

This book will give you food for thought for your own garden or patio. Of any aspect of gardening, growing plants in containers is perhaps the greatest fun. It is mobile, flexible and adaptable – and you can achieve an almost instant effect and transform any outdoor area, however small, into a stylish, easy to maintain environment in which to relax.

*Yvonne Rees and David Palliser,*
*Bryn Hill Cottage, Bishop's Castle.*

# Introduction

Displaying plants in pots and containers offers many opportunities to transform the garden, patio or terrace almost instantly. You can try out new ideas and combinations without major reconstruction or landscaping work and, under the semi-controlled conditions a container can provide, it can be the only way to enjoy some of your favourite plants where the site may be unsuitable or the weather unkind. Anywhere with a hard, firm surface is likely to benefit from the softening or invigorating effect of a show of foliage or bright blooms. Containers add a different dimension to gardening and it is hardly surprising that they have become so popular, not only for plant lovers with little more than a square of city concrete to play with, but also for owners of bigger gardens, who are attracted by extra design possibilities and the benefits of low maintenance.

Despite the fact that plants confined to containers require more careful feeding and watering than those in the garden, they are remarkably easy to control and look after once you recognise their needs and organise yourself to meet them. Soil tends to dry out quickly and watering must be regularly maintained, particularly for trees and shrubs in pots, although mulching with moss, bark chips, or small pebbles can help to reduce moisture loss. Since its roots are unable to travel any further than the confines of the pot, the container-grown plant will also require feeding for healthy growth once it has exhausted the goodness of the existing compost (see page 77 for details).

The little care and organisation necessary to keep plants in good condition is far outweighed by the advantages of container gardening.

These include the visual potential of combining different styles of pot and plant groupings; the cleanliness and convenience of gardening with sterilised soil, neatly contained by a pot or tub; and, once the plants are established, there is no digging or re-shaping and virtually no weeding to do. As the container garden is usually sited on a patio, terrace or similar paved surface, it also provides dry, clean access so that the area can be enjoyed all year round and in all weathers. Plants

Fig 4    Taking a pink and mauve colour theme, these identical containers have been grouped at different heights to create a special effect in the garden.

7

grown in tubs or pots are much appreciated by disabled gardeners, since the extra height and easy maintenance makes them more accessible.

Since the gardener has control over the plants' environment, it is possible to grow species with very specific soil requirements even if the soil in your garden is completely unsuitable. Containers are a means of growing favourite plants such as azaleas, rhododendrons, heathers and other lime haters in predominantly chalk sites. A collection of plants with a particular theme can also be developed, since it is so much easier to control the group's requirements. You could construct a small alpine garden in a trough of stony soil, a display of exotics that can be taken under cover at the end of the summer, and so on.

You can keep a display of plants in pots looking good all year as it is easy to replant and replace specimens when past their best or if they fail. Maintaining seasonal interest could not

*Fig 5   An ornamental foliage plant creates the effect of a fountain, planted in this reconstituted stone urn.*

be more convenient or exciting; plants can be forced in pots under cover and added to the arrangement when coming up to bloom, and fresh varieties can be added or subtracted at a whim. This is gardening which is mobile and completely flexible. You can change your ideas as frequently as you do your indoor accessories and even take the whole thing with you if you move house. Easy-care and interchangeable, this is very much the gardening style for today.

## POTS FROM THE PAST

Container-grown plants have been around for as long as man has made gardens. Earthenware and terracotta pots for flowers, shrubs, herbs and small fruit trees, little changed in shape from the ones we have today, were certainly used by the Romans and ancient Greeks; special pots for growing lemon trees are mentioned by Pliny the Elder. The Chinese used beautiful glazed ceramic containers for flowering plants and shrubs, sometimes supported on stands, as early as the 7th century AD. By medieval times, a wide variety of shapes and sizes (including window-boxes) were available, mostly made of terracotta. Gradually, improved skills in working other materials led to decorative stone, lead and timber tubs and urns for displaying citrus trees and showy flowering shrubs being produced.

In the early 19th century when the Victorians were mass producing flower pots, saucers appeared, and were accompanied by highly ornate shapes and styles of earthenware and metal containers. The metal jardinière for displaying several plants was also developed. Many Victorian containers survive and are eagerly sought for today's container gardens. A genuine antique will add a sense of maturity and timelessness to a traditional-style patio or terrace.

The newer pots satisfy all tastes and styles from rustic Mediterranean terracotta to glazed oriental jars, with faithful reproductions of historic styles and modern, easy-care cement and fibreglass.

# POTS ON DISPLAY

## Patios

Without tubs and pots of plants, a patio looks very stark. A successful display here relies on good grouping and choice of plants in containers, on a sound, level surface. It is worth making sure that the patio itself is well constructed or that an existing area is in a good condition, especially if you intend to plant more permanent pot-grown features like climbers up an adjoining wall or trellis. Check also that the patio surface is level and well laid.

The choice of paving materials is wide and should complement your containers as the background on which they stand. Hard materials available include many colours and textures, from natural stone paving to shaped concrete pavers and bricks, all of which can be laid in a variety of decorative patterns. Mixing materials can work extremely well providing you do not try to combine more than two or three different types. A change of texture or colour could indicate planting areas, but be practical – pots may not stand level on a stretch of cobbles, although a square of gravel would be fine and provide good drainage.

Timber makes a softer and increasingly popular surface in the garden. Planks supported by wooden posts can be arranged to create raised decking, a couple of inches off the ground or higher if required, to accommodate a change of level, adjoin the house or overhang an ornamental pool. Timber raised more than 45cm (18in) off the ground should be fitted with a safety rail. Planks can be laid in a variety of decorative patterns and may be of softwood such as deal or pine, which needs regular maintenance, or a hardwood like western red cedar or chestnut. Decking can be designed to incorporate changes of level to display plant containers on raised platforms or in sunken areas. It would be possible to construct such a design with paving, but working with timber makes it easier and less expensive to be creative.

Fig 6 *Containers can be used to add seasonal colour to a small garden or patio maintaining a strong framework of background greenery.*

You can stain or varnish the decking in any shade of natural brown, dark blue, green or Chinese red stains; bleaching the timber grey, cream or white to soften it and thereby produce a pleasant weather-worn effect is also popular.

The position and use of a patio area will influence the type of container you choose and the plants you put in it. Traditionally enclosed on three or four sides, a patio is frequently a sun-trap offering the chance to grow some really brightly blooming or fruiting sun lovers. Beware of patios in full sun which can dry out plants too quickly causing them to wilt or leaves

Fig 7  *Standard trees clipped into ornamental shapes look perfect in pairs when arranged in formal containers on either side of a flight of steps, doorway or other special garden feature.*

and buds to drop. It makes sense to select sun-loving annuals, alpines, roses and many of the silver foliaged plants; and take special care over watering, particularly your hanging baskets. A pergola structure clothed in climbers, built-in awnings or blinds can help filter strong sunshine and provide welcome shade for both plants and people.

The patio might be bordered on one side by the house or, to catch maximum sunshine, at the far end of the garden, sometimes positioned in front of a small summerhouse or chalet. It is likely to be a place for relaxing on comfortable furniture or for having a barbecue, so you will be looking for sweet scented plants, bright summer flowers, and aromatic herbs like rosemary for popping straight on to the grill with your steaks and chops.

Where the area is close by the house, maintain some sense of continuity, especially if your rooms open directly on to the garden via patio doors or French windows, by choosing containers to match the style of accessories indoors.

## Basements

A basement or small enclosed backyard could be dark, dank and shady. Here it is important to liven up tall and imposing walls or fencing and the vertical surfaces may offer more scope than the rather cramped paved area below (*see* page 27). Shade-tolerant climbing plants such as honeysuckle and some clematis hybrids can also be grown in containers and are useful for smothering large areas of dull wall in leaves and flowers. Brighten up a shady area with tubs of begonias, feathery ferns, shrubs like winter jasmine and cheery spring bulbs. Painting a tall wall white or cream helps add a little light and makes a good background for your plants.

## Terraces and Verandahs

Another place where you will find plants grown exclusively in containers is along a terrace or a verandah. Usually a fairly narrow, paved area, the verandah is distinguished by some kind of roof, frequently glass, sometimes with glazed sections at the front and sides. Ornamental trees and shrubs are traditionally ranged along the back wall in boxes or decorative pots, and the covered verandah receiving plenty of sunshine is an excellent place to indulge in a few tender exotics like the European fan palm, a dwarf banana, or a pretty orange tree. If the area is unheated, tender species could be overwintered in a light position indoors.

## Passages and Pools

It is often possible to brighten up a gloomy side passage with tubs of shade-tolerant plants such as ivies, ferns and hostas or a succession of bright annuals that can be changed as they start to fade. Pots also look good and are one of the most practical options around a pool. Lush moisture-loving species like hostas, rush or dramatic bamboo do well in pots which help to keep foliage and soil out of the water and prevent it becoming polluted. You can stand them on a spread of shingle or on timber decking around an informal pool; or on the flat-topped coving of a formal pool.

*Fig 8    Raise small containers on benches and tables to give them prominence.*

*Fig 9    Wall baskets are useful for decorating dull areas.*

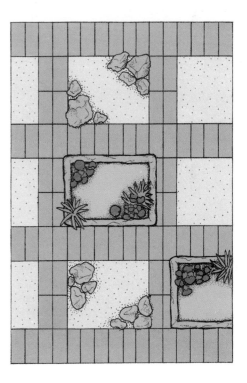

*Fig 10    Container water garden. Even the smallest paved area can enjoy a few fish, water plants or water-lilies by turning an old stone sink or similar container into a miniature raised pool.*

11

*Fig 11  Some containers can be adapted into small water gardens, like this tiny bubble fountain playing over an arrangement of pebbles.*

## Roof Gardens

On a roof garden, plants in tubs or pots are usually the only option as soil beds of sufficient depth would be too weighty and laborious to construct and maintain. Depending on the permitted loading – an architect will be necessary to advise here – everything needs to be lightweight including your containers which should be predominantly of fibreglass, plastic or wood, rather than heavy stone or metal. A light, peat-based compost also helps save on weight.

However, roof gardens tend to be extremely exposed to wind and weather, so take care that containers cannot blow over. Screens to protect both plants and pots can be made of reinforced glass and acrylic plastic, which will not impede your views, but they are slippery and not suitable for climbing plants. Wire mesh, wooden or bamboo trellis may be more attractive, providing a more intimate enclosure and offering better protection and improved resistance to wind damage than a solid screen.

The roof garden can also be cruelly prone to exposure from strong sunlight above. A retractable awning or a timber pergola structure will help provide solid or filtered shade. Hardier plants such as tough creepers like virginia creeper, trailers like honeysuckle and ivies, or hardy shrubs like broom, gorse, juniper and heathers, with bulbs and annual flowers for seasonal interest, will survive such extremes.

In busy cities it may be a good idea to select plants that have some resistance to pollution as levels are bound to be increased at height – viburnum is a suitable choice.

Best distribution of weight is normally achieved by placing the majority of containers around the edges of the roof garden, unless you know where the supporting crossbeams are. Equal care should be given to the weight of paving material and sections of lightweight timber decking are ideal for this, particularly since they can normally just be laid down on the existing surface and lifted or removed as required, with no preparation work necessary. However, tiles

*Fig 12    An arrangement of shrubs and trees in containers can transform a flat roof into a pleasant garden.*

*Fig 13    Bamboo screening and glazed pots of glossy* Fatsia japonica *have created a secluded roof garden with an oriental atmosphere.*

or light pavers are also practical and highly decorative – and, like timber sections, relatively easy to transfer on to the roof.

You must also consider how you are going to water your plants as they may need attention as often as twice a day in hot weather owing to the higher rate of evaporation. A tap or hose connection makes more sense than carrying up heavy buckets of water from down below. Care will need to be taken that water is not allowed to spill over and stand on the roof; you may have to use saucers or drip troughs beneath your containers.

If you are considering constructing a new roof garden, it would be a good idea to check on any planning restrictions and to ask the advice of a qualified architect on the load-bearing capacity of your roof before you make any structural alterations.

## Balconies

A balcony presents similar problems to a roof garden in that it tends to be exposed to sun and wind and can only take lightweight features. They are normally rather narrow so even the use of containers will be restricted, particularly if you wish to add a couple of chairs and a table. Climbing or twining plants are usually given priority, grown in tubs and persuaded to clothe the sides of the balcony area screened by trellis – ivy, climbing hydrangea, honeysuckle or vines do well. Or for a more exotic effect in a warm, sheltered location, try a passion flower, or Chinese gooseberry.

Use only the lightest pots and paving and take great care when watering to avoid any kind of overspill which might cause damage below. A balcony is designed to look good

13

Fig 14   Use tubs of plants to brighten up a dull series of steps.

from the ground as well as from above, so flowering perennials and bright annuals are often displayed in window-boxes or hanging baskets attached to the balcony rails; or a prolific flowering trailer such as nasturtium, lobelia or trailing carnation can be planted in troughs on the balcony. Apartments with a sunny, sheltered balcony can even grow a few edible plants; a tub of tiny cherry tomatoes or a hanging basket of strawberries will ripen nicely and are unlikely to be raided by birds.

## Front of House

Pots are a good choice for the front of the house which has to take a lot of wear and tear with people coming in and out and the stress of passing traffic. Pots offer some protection from accidental trampling, cats, dogs and carelessly-left bicycles. Pollution can be resolved by changing the soil or replacing ailing plants if necessary. Deciduous plants generally stand up to pollution better than evergreens, while plants with thick, soft hairy foliage are susceptible to damage from soot and petrol fumes. Growing plants close together in groups helps them to survive by creating their own miniature environment.

You will find that spring bulbs, alpines, delicate aquilegias, perennial flax and day lilies are all tough town dwellers. You could also safely plant indestructible elephant's ears (*Bergenia*), roses, crab apple and cherry trees, forsythia, and buddleia, a plant so resistant you can see it thriving in the crevices of soot-stained railway walls. Plants at the front of the house should give a cheery welcome to visitors, so go for an interesting background of foliage plants, bright or scented blooms and a well-planned succession of seasonal colour using bulbs and annuals.

*Fig 15   A magnificent reproduction antique stone urn makes an excellent centre-piece to display seasonal plants.*

A pair of matching pots or urns transforms an entrance and with a couple of fine trees or shrubs it can look quite grand. The effect tends to be formal with containers raised on a pedestal or standing either side of the door or gateway, or flanking a flight of steps down from a patio into the garden. It is important that the paired plants match closely in size, shape and condition to maintain the formal effect. These sentinel plants might include clipped topiary shapes in box or yew, a shaped standard such as bay, rose or marguerite, or, for year-round interest, any decorative shrub with a distinct shape and tidy habit.

Fig 16   Use containers round the pool to keep invasive marginal plants in check.

## The Main Garden

Pots also have their place in the main garden. Raised on a pedestal, they may be positioned as the central point of a lawn or of paving in a formal feature such as a rose or herb garden. Alternatively you might see a fine specimen shrub or a sudden flash of seasonal colour in a decorative urn at the end of a path or vista to create a focal point. Pots of spring bulbs, summer annuals and tender specimens like some fruit trees which have been forced or wintered indoors, can be brought out and positioned where they will add highlights to your more permanent scheme. A row of ornamental trees or shrubs in matching pots could be ranged alongside a formal path to present an attractive summer walkway. Small pots of herbs and flowers could be arranged in groups on garden tables, benches, steps and windowsills.

Fig 17   Pretty Mimulus and a trailing ivy have decorated a hanging basket which will look good all year round.

Look for other possible nooks and crannies; along the edge of a flat-roofed shed or garage; at any point where the garden changes level; or where a dull corner needs brightening up or softening down. A simple shelf built round a mature tree trunk or other permanent feature makes a fine place to stand a collection of small pots of herbs or flowering plants.

Do use hanging baskets in the garden if you want to add the attraction of trailing plants or a mass of summer colour at eye level. Attach them to garden buildings like sheds and chalets to disguise or soften their outline – a useful device for small gardens; hang them from sturdy pergola structures or attach to special poles anywhere in the garden; pair them up for greater impact on either side of a path, gateway or entrance.

# CHAPTER 1

# Tubs, Troughs, Pots and Baskets

## CHOOSING CONTAINERS

For both visual and practical reasons, your choice of container is as important as the plants that will go in it and every pot should be selected for its decorative impact as carefully as any interior accessory. Size and shape must be your first consideration, bearing in mind not only the plant's practical needs, but also how the pot or group of pots are going to look planted up *in situ*.

Large containers are expensive, but it would be a false economy to cut down on the size (or quality) of a certain container simply to suit a stringent budget. Plants may look overcrowded or quickly outgrow their pot; or the containers may look lost and ridiculous in position. Ideally, you should estimate the correct-sized container for the plant's proposed growth over the next couple of seasons. Too big a pot can be as bad as too little for perennial plants such as shrubs and trees as they will not make good growth if

*Fig 18   Tubs of summer flowering plants used to add height and interest in the garden.*

Fig 19    Here different shapes of pot are grouped together for an effect of profusion, flanking a stone bench.

given too much room. Fast-growing annuals can be crammed in slightly to produce an effect of lush profusion and a mass of shapes and colours. Again, you will have to calculate how large and how quickly plants will grow to estimate how

Fig 20    A cast-iron trough will give a Victorian feel to the surroundings.

many you need. Different shapes and colours can be cleverly combined within a single container; or a specimen plant such as a good foliage subject like a fern or hosta, or an individual tree or shrub, can be planted separately and given a pot to itself. Make sure the container complements the specimen plant – a bamboo in a glazed oriental urn for example, or a clipped bay tree in a formal painted Versailles tub.

## Pot Sizes

The standard terracotta clay pot comes in a huge selection of sizes from a diameter of around 5cm (2in) up to 45–60cm (18–24in). The smallest sizes are not really suitable for plants on display, unless you are planning a miniature garden. Generally, the 15cm (6in) size is the minimum you should be considering, particularly as the soil in anything smaller than this tends to dry out very quickly. Certainly,

Fig 21    Low troughs can be useful for collections of small-leaved or trailing plants. These stone containers attractively imitate an old-fashioned mill wheel.

Fig 22    Terracotta containers come in a wide range of styles for different plant needs.

permanent plants such as shrubs, trees, climbers and perennials should not be planted in a container any smaller than this. You need a soil depth of at least 30cm (12in) for growing foliage shrubs as background greenery.

These days, containers come in all kinds of materials and sizes, but you will find that they are mainly based on the old traditional pots. Tubs and planters tend to be used for larger plants and the most popular size for a wooden or concrete tub is around 40–50cm (16–20in) across by 35–45cm (14–18in) high. Larger still, for planning groups of plants or miniature gardens, are planters with a depth of around 45–60cm (18–24in) to provide plenty of room for roots to grow and for better moisture retention in warm weather.

Containers need not be purpose made, as we shall see, and sizes vary considerably. It is interesting to vary both sizes and heights within a scheme, not just to suit individual plant require-

19

Fig 23   These pretty terracotta baskets are perfect for a collection of
small-leaved foliage plants in a shady corner of the patio.

ments, but also to provide variety among your pots. Old barrels and chimney pots are useful taller containers; shallow troughs and saucers are excellent for trailing plants or alpines at ground level or displayed on a bench, shelf or table-top. Shallow clay pots called pans, and half-height pots are available for low-growing plants which can look out of proportion in full-height containers. Wider shallow bowls can be used for your flowering annuals if they are deep enough – about 23–30cm (9–12in) should be sufficient.

Some special containers are available for particular plants. Strawberry barrels and towers, which can be used for growing a large amount of fruit in the minimum of space, are also useful for bedding plants and alpines should you want to create a multi-tiered display. Strawberry tubs generally come in two heights: 60cm (24in) to hold 30 plants, or 84cm (33in) high to hold 50 plants. Tubs take up only 0.2sq m (2.25 sq ft) of

your patio or garden. Operating on a similar principal, but smaller, are 'parsley pots' which are perfect for any collection of trailing plants, alpines or small-leaved herbs. These stand around 30–40cm (12–16in) high. You will probably be considering a couple of hanging baskets too, to add height to your planting scheme and these usually come in two sizes with a diameter of 20cm (8in) or 30–45cm (12–18in). Depth of basket tends to vary between 15–23cm (6–9in).

## Pot Shapes and Styles

With such a wide range of containers to choose from, style, colour and shape can be selected to suit not just the plant, but also to fit in with the general atmosphere of your patio or garden and the style of your home. Where pots are to be positioned on a patio, balcony or terrace adjoining the house and linked visually to the rooms inside by plate-glass windows or patio doors, matching the general style of your containers to your interior scheme and accessories creates a pleasing sense of continuity and an impression of space, especially if you can also continue your paving right through from indoors to out.

Materials available for your outdoor pots include traditional clay, wood, metal, concrete, plastic, stone, fibreglass and glazed ceramic, each of which has its own decorative appeal and will help create a certain atmosphere. Earthy terracotta seems to invoke the warmth of the Mediterranean, while glazed Chinese ginger jars suggest the Orient, particularly if planted with a bamboo or similarly dramatic foliage plant. Generally, a mixed arrangement of containers is far more successful if you combine different heights, shapes and designs within a certain style, rather than mixing materials which can look bitty and confusing. If you do want to add some variety – and the contrast of textures between materials such as rough timber or clay against sleek plastic or glossy glazed pots can be worth exploiting – never combine more than two types within a single scheme and try to group at least two or three containers of a single type together in different areas rather than mixing singles.

Another point to consider when selecting your containers is their durability. A glazed finish is fine on a sheltered patio or balcony, but on an exposed site or roof garden, you are better advised to choose something which will withstand hard frost. Clay and concrete are sturdy, and some are specially treated to survive cold conditions, so do check before you buy. You should also bear in mind when buying timber or metal containers that, while they stand up to weather reasonably well, they will also need a certain amount of regular maintenance such as rubbing down and re-painting or priming.

The traditional terracotta flower pot can be plain or patterned with a simple tooled design or horizontal band, or an elaborate, applied decoration – perhaps classical heads, figures or

Fig 24    The natural discoloration and mossy growth on terracotta containers is often considered a plus point for its mellowing effect.

flowers. Colours can vary, according to the firing and some pots are oxidised to produce an uneven darkening which is instantly mellowing and creates an almost antiqued effect. Terracotta may be plain or glazed, but always retains

Fig 25    A simple arrangement of interlocked timber makes a fine low, lightweight container for bedding plants on the roof garden or patio.

21

Fig 26    Terracotta pots come in a wide range of shapes and styles from plain garden pots and bowls to decorated urns and wall pots.

Fig 27    Classical style boxes and troughs can be made in wood or tough fibreglass which requires no maintenance and does not rot.

that rough, rustic feel. The tops of pots may be sloped slightly inwards or outwards and have a flat ring or curved lip. Other styles include the wide-topped, old-fashioned citrus pots, designed for orange and lemon trees in the days when orangeries were popular, and these make good containers for hardy shrubs as well as ornamental trees. An advantage of clay pots is that they are heavy so are less likely to overbalance with large or heavy plants. However, they can chip or crack if mishandled; and those which are not guaranteed frost-resistant may not survive the winter unscathed. Because the material is porous, compost dries out quickly, particularly in hot weather, so you will need to remember to water frequently. Clay pots are also prone to a mossy growth which is difficult to clean off, but some people like the aged effect this produces.

The mellow, natural effect of clay suits all kinds of plants as does timber, with its attractive grain and worn, natural colouring. You can buy custom-made timber containers, either metal-bound circular tubs for an informal garden or the classic square boxes called Versailles tubs,

Fig 28    Maintenance-free fibreglass troughs and planters are available in a range of sizes and decorative patterns and are perfect for roof gardens and balconies because of their relative lightness.

panelled with neat finial decorations, which are perfect for standard trees such as bay, rose or citrus, and for decorative shrubs like hydrangeas. Traditionally, the panels at the side are removable so that the compost can be easily replaced when its nutrients are exhausted. Versailles tubs can be stained and varnished but are more usually painted in white or cream. However, the introduction of coloured wood glazes has encouraged a more adventurous approach and tubs may now be stained a soft blue, green or grey to add interest without hiding the grain of the timber.

Any suitable wooden receptacle can be pressed into service as a plant container, and wooden tubs and barrels, usually bound by iron hoops, are most popular and quite cheaply available. Large barrels are useful for displaying larger specimen shrubs and trees for permanent planting, but since smaller plants, unless they are of a trailing variety, look rather out of proportion, barrels are often sawn in half horizontally to make a more manageable container. You should check that the barrel has not been used to store toxic liquids and that the timber joints are tight enough not to let out too much moisture. Treating inside and out with a non-toxic preservative (not creosote which is poisonous to plants), helps to seal timber and

delay rot. Holes drilled in the base will improve drainage; alternatively, convert a sound, waterproof barrel into a small patio pool complete with fish and water-lilies.

Because they are large and deep, timber tubs and barrels are ideally suited to displaying the bigger, permanant plants such as trees, shrubs and climbers; they will also keep compost moist for longer so are recommended for plants in a particularly hot, dry situation. It is a good idea to raise them up a couple of inches on blocks of

Fig 29    The traditional wooden tub is bound in metal for a suitably rustic look.

wood or bricks to avoid contact between the timber and the ground, and to improve drainage.

Stone is another natural material that looks good with most types of plant. However, stone urns and pots are expensive and heavy so they are normally only found in smaller sizes and are therefore only suited to smaller plants. It is possible to find decorative antique stone containers in good condition but they are quite expensive and deserve pride of place as the focal point of a formal garden or patio. More readily available are reconstituted stone pots and tubs which can be relatively inexpensive depending on quality and finish, and are usually designed in imitation of the best original styles. Old lead planters which tend to be decorated in relief with classical themes and are highly attractive in an old-fashioned formal garden, either painted or in a natural weathered grey, can sometimes be found in specialist salvage yards and auctions. Again, faithful reproductions are available; Queen Anne urns and Georgian-style tubs, Adam window-boxes and large, ornate water tanks, perfect for use as a permanent bed for shrubs and perennials.

Modern materials such as concrete, plastic or fibreglass offer an equally wide range of strong, easy-care options, mostly based on familiar tub and pot shapes, sizes and designs. Concrete has the advantage of being cheap and, painted white with a rough cast finish, is attractive enough as a no-nonsense, plain container once planted up. Better quality, glass-reinforced cement is completely frost-proof and can be scrubbed down without damaging the surface – an important factor for city backyards or front gardens where traffic pollution can quickly discolour containers. Custom-designed to create interesting groups of different sizes, shapes and heights, you will find an excellent choice of circular, square and rectangular containers from shallow bowls to tubular columns, all in reinforced cement. Plastic and fibreglass are lightweight and frost-proof making them ideal for roof gardens and balconies. Most frequently seen are large square or rectangular planters, suitable for displaying a range of different plants in small backyards or on roof gardens where there are no areas of natural soil. Like tubs and barrels, planters are better raised a few inches off the ground to

*Fig 30   Ornamental urns are a splendid addition to a formal terrace and are available as authentic copies of classical styles like this reproduction of a Victorian original, itself imitating Greek design.*

Fig 31 (a)–(d)   There is a variety of glazed or terracotta pots and urns which can be used to co-ordinate or diversify a display of plants and flowers.

improve drainage. Also useful for a mixed plant arrangement and for providing a change of size and shape within your display, are plant troughs, available in timber, concrete, clay, fibreglass or stone. Again, these can be plain or ornate, standing at ground level on bricks or wooden blocks for good drainage, or arranged on a low wall or bench.

Where the edges between interior and exterior design have become a bit blurred and you are hoping to create a sophisticated, garden 'room', maybe opening off from one of the rooms of the house, more ornamental containers are available for frost-free situations. Glazed terracotta and ceramic is very stylish and comes in an increasing choice of shapes and patterns, often hand painted. Large, glazed Mediterranean oil jars with narrow necks, or elegant Chinese ginger jars can be planted up with the appropriate style of plant to create a certain atmosphere. Sometimes such beautiful containers almost take on the role of garden sculpture and are left empty, positioned among simpler pots of plants like an accessory, perhaps matched to similar containers indoors. This is worth considering for narrow-necked urns and jars which, although highly attractive, are only really suited to smaller trailing plants, but make excellent focal points unplanted, raised on a low wall, pedestal or similar support.

If you like a highly original effect, it is worth keeping an eye open for suitable 'found' containers for your plants; any which are not waterproof or which have insufficient drainage can still be put to good use by growing your specimens in ordinary clay or plastic garden pots and standing them inside your box, basket or other container with a saucer or tray of gravel for drainage. The above-mentioned barrels, large baskets (they need not be in particularly good condition – an old sea-tossed fisherman's basket or broken lobster pot could look great in the right setting), and wooden crates or boxes treated to a dose of preservative and a coat of varnish or paint, all make interesting, informal plant containers. Other

Fig 32   Look out for unusual containers like this tin bath, given a new lease of life as a hanging basket with a coat of paint and a collection of bright annuals.

popular conversions include small baths, old sinks, and cisterns which can be neatly disguised by covering with rough mortar and painting white. Mix two parts peat to one part sand and one part cement with water and apply to your container about 1·3cm (0·5in) thick. Where the surface is highly glazed, a primary coat of resin adhesive will improve the grip of your mortar mixture. An old chimney pot also makes an elegant, tall plant container or a pedestal support for a shallow bowl or dish in matching terracotta planted with a trailing plant such as ivy, lobelia or fuchsia. Look out for other unsual containers that could be put to good use; an old leaky watering can, cooking pot or painted metal bucket might all make a stylish home to a small plant.

## Purely Functional

So far we have looked at the more attractive options among plant containers for using creatively in the garden or on the patio. Most are practical enough for plants to be grown safely and successfully directly in the pot or tub. However, you may need inexpensive, purely functional pots for plant raising or for temporary, seasonal plants to be inserted in a more decorative container and replaced as and when required. Clay pots fall more or less into both categories – they are highly suited to propagation, yet they retain a certain rough charm which means that they are not obtrusive if kept on view.

The modern alternative to clay pots is plastic, and these are available in an equal number of shapes and sizes, in a passable terracotta colour or black. Plastic pots are cheap and hold moisture well so are good for raising plants that like damp conditions. They are not suitable for species which prefer good drainage and can be a little too light and fragile for big specimen plants, exposed conditions or rough handling. If you are raising your own plants, particularly vegetables, the most inexpensive and practical choice is peat pots which allow the roots to grow right through the sides enabling the plant to be planted on with minimum disturbance – the only disadvantage is that the compost tends to dry out quickly so needs careful watering while the plant is young. 'Whalehide' paper pots are used in the same way as peat pots for starting off plants and black polythene bags are also a useful and inexpensive way to grow your own summer annuals and vegetables. The plastic is simply slit around the root ball and carefully pulled off when you need to plant out.

Grow-bags, narrow polythene bags of soil-less compost and nutrients, are popular for growing fruits and vegetables on patios, balconies and terraces. Measuring about 1·2m (4ft) long they are lightweight and highly successful, providing you purchase a recommended brand. However, they are not very attractive and the bags are better disguised with a low wall of stones or bricks, or dropped into an appropriate-sized trough if you are trying to maintain a stylish atmosphere. If drainage is a problem on a roof garden or balcony, the bag can be placed on a tray of gravel to prevent water damage.

*Fig 33    Pots of flowering plants can be attached to walls and fences on wires and trellis for extra seasonal display.*

## VERTICAL GARDENING

It is particularly important to add height to the container garden, especially in the backyard or roof garden where everything can be rather ground-based, providing little of interest above waist height and even allowing the effect to be spoiled by less than attractive surroundings. The backyard or basement area is often dull and oppressive, hemmed in by high walls or surrounding buildings to produce a rather claustrophobic, depressing effect. The opposite

27

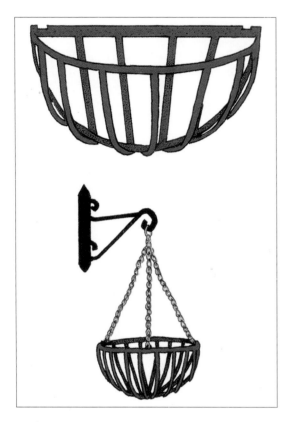

*Fig 34    The traditional hay rack style basket is normally made of wrought iron and makes a fine wall-hung container that is easily removed for winter storage.*

should also be climbers – distinctive foliage or flowering species like clematis, honeysuckle, vines and ornamental ivies – trained up nearby trellis, along wires fastened to the walls or to a special freestanding column or screen with supports made of black nylon-coated tubing which look like old-fashioned wrought iron and can be inserted into the container.

However, some containers are specially designed to be fastened to walls, fences and trellis to provide a vertical display of foliage and flowers. Because it is container-based, this can be changed with the seasons or from year to year with the introduction of new varieties, colours and shapes.

Window-boxes can do much to brighten up a building, both front and rear, where a seasonal display of blooms will add life to the immediate area around the house and also provides a fine view from indoors. For some, the window-box is all the garden they have and this may be several storeys up, yet it still provides the pleasures of gardening in miniature. The box should be firmly attached to the wall of the house with strong wrought iron brackets. The ideal dimensions are for the box to equal the width of the sill from front to back plus an

*Fig 35    A profusion of superb foliage shapes and colours have here created an unusual window display.*

problem is encountered with a roof garden; there is a need to relieve that overpowering feeling of vertigo, of being exposed to the sky and all the elements. Screens, supports and climbing plants are essential to create a cosier, more secluded atmosphere and to protect more tender plants from the ravages of unrelieved wind and sun.

Small trees and shrubs in pots and tubs are an obvious choice to add variety of height and shape to your scheme; but there are other ingenious means of introducing something of interest above waist and shoulder level. Ornamental pots and urns can be placed on matching stone or terracotta pedestals; troughs and pots supported by low walls or shelves. There

overlap of 2.5cm (1in). It should be tilted slightly backwards using wedges under the front edge. On narrow sills or where brackets are not practical, the box can be supported from above by strong ties. The boxes should be at least 23cm (9in) deep to ensure that the soil does not dry out too quickly. Drainage holes can be a nuisance, especially where the window-boxes are sited on an upper level, and unless a drip tray is incorporated (and never allowed to overfill), a good layer of small stones, gravel and broken crocks in the bottom of the container should be sufficient if you water carefully. Add a layer of moss to help hold the moisture, then top up with a loamless potting mixture which is lightweight, clean to handle and does not dry out too quickly. Window-boxes tend to be rather exposed, so moisture retention and regular watering are important. Since you will probably be planting fast-gowing seasonal plants, they will be greedy feeders and existing nutrients in the compost may be quickly exhausted, so feed regularly during the growing season with a recommended fertiliser and replace the soil completely annually.

A clever idea is to grow your plants in inner liners made of metal or plastic and usually incorporating drainage holes, to be inserted within the main protective and decorative box. The advantage of this arrangement is that the liners can be removed for thorough soaking should they dry out; or taken down while you are away on holiday and left with a friend or put in a shadier part of the garden. You might also like to maintain two liners per box, planting up a new display to be ready as soon as the one *in situ* starts to go over. The alternative is to position plants directly in the compost or to leave them in their pots and pack round them with damp peat.

You could construct your own window-boxes out of timber, designed to fit your sills exactly and painted or stained and varnished to suit the style of your house exterior. Window-boxes are also readily available in terracotta, aluminium, concrete, plastic and fibreglass.

*Fig 36    Geraniums make perfect plants for window-boxes with their combination of interesting flowers and foliage.*

Timber containers should be made of a durable hardwood such as teak or redwood, while softwoods such as pine need to be treated with a non-toxic preservative inside and out before planting.

Plants can be chosen as external decoration; a succession of flowering bulbs in spring, bright annuals in summer and appropriate evergreens to last through the winter. You should dead-head and replace plants as required to keep the display looking fresh and in peak condition. You could alternatively relate the contents of your window-box to the room inside with a permanent display of light, leafy foliage plants to screen a bathroom window, or a selection of herbs outside the kitchen. Window-boxes need not be restricted to the main building however; they look equally good fastened to the top of a wall with strong brackets, along the edge of a flat-roofed garage or shed planted with flowering trailers, or decorating the windows of a shed, summerhouse or chalet elsewhere in the garden.

Hanging baskets are even more versatile.

29

*Fig 37    Glazed terracotta wall pots make a colourful vertical display.*

They can be fixed at any level on your house wall or the side of a shed, wall or summer-house, and can also add height to the garden, by affixing to a pergola or trellis structure; or be completely freestanding on either side of a path or seating area, on special supported poles. Planted with a carefully planned mass of foliage plants, flowers and trailers, a hanging basket will brighten any dull expanse of wall or trellis and provide interest without taking up space below. Correctly maintained they can look quite spendid, singly or in pairs to frame an entrance or doorway; or *en masse* as a real eye-catcher. Hanging baskets do need a little care to keep them looking good, because they are so exposed, particularly around the roots.

You may like to get your plants well established under glass before putting the basket in position for an instant effect; but never hang outdoors while there is still a risk of frost. The compost tends to dry out rapidly and may need watering twice a day. This is not always an easy task, particularly if the compost has dried out too much in which case a waterfall will tumble on to your head. A solution to this is to lift down the baskets and stand them in a tub of water until bubbles cease. Ideally, you should use a small watering can with a long spout so that you can reach right into the middle of the basket and there is even a special device designed for watering hanging baskets, comprising a hand pump with a long plastic tube. For safety, you should also check periodically that the basket supports are sound; strong chains and hooks are best.

The baskets themselves can be made of plastic-coated galvanised wire, terracotta, wooden slats or plastic with integral drip tray and a choice of colours. Choice depends on your style of garden and personal tastes. A similar range of wall baskets is available which are very useful where space is strictly limited or where a hanging basket would not be conven-ient, such as a windy site or on a wall in a very narrow area such as a side passage. These are more like half-baskets or metal 'hay racks' and are fastened directly to a wall, trellis or other permanent screen or support and, again, can be planted up with a good variety of different foliage and flower shapes and colours, designed to smother the basket almost completely with a profusion of plant material.

Another good way to cover a high wall or trellis surrounding a backyard garden, balcony or roof garden, is to attach many small pots of plants to the vertical surface until it is virtually covered. Clay or plastic pots can be fixed with wires or ties for an inexpensive but effective display. Plants can be removed and replaced as required and, again, should be well watered under such exposed conditions. If it is not acceptable for the water to drain on to the

*Fig 38   Group small pots of different foliage shapes together, raising some on steps or staging to produce a three-dimensional effect.*

surface below, you should use pots with built-in saucers.

Another clever idea to provide a vertical display is a mobile plant 'wall' comprising a wooden frame covered in chicken wire and filled with peat or moss into which plants are inserted through the wires to produce, in time, a solid mass of foliage and flowers. If you mount the structure on casters it can be moved into position wherever you need it to provide privacy, shelter or an interesting but lightweight display on the balcony, patio or roof garden. The display can be one-sided with a solid back, or two-sided, as required, and should be fitted with a drip tray within the base. A two-sided display must be around 25–30cm (10–12in) deep between the layers of wire. Treat the wooden framework and solid base with non-toxic preservative and cover with 5cm (2in) mesh. When drip tray and casters are fitted, fill with damp peat or sphagnum moss then insert a variety of small plants about 10–13cm (4in) apart between the mesh, press the compost round the roots and water in thoroughly. Never allow the compost to dry out completely and feed regularly through the growing season; about once a week for a moss wall, or every two weeks for peat.

## POSITIONING YOUR POTS

Containers should be put in their final position before planting while they are not so heavy and are thus easier to move around. You will probably have to experiment with grouping pots together until they look right from the point of view of height, shape, style and compatibility. Odd numbers of pots always seem to look better than even ones and can be positioned in triangular arrangements, which are perfect for corners. If you are working with very large containers, it may be advisable to work out your design roughly on paper first to save too many back-breaking alterations. When the containers are in a satisfactory position, walk round them and view the arrangement from all angles, from house and garden or even from upstairs, if it helps you see the plan more easily. Only when you are sure you have the positions exactly right should you start filling with compost and planting them up.

Pots and tubs should be placed directly on a hard level surface, supported by wooden blocks if you wish to improve drainage. In the garden or on the patio, standing porous containers such as clay pots on areas of pebbles or gravel will help retain moisture, and these could be incorporated into your main paving plan. For

Fig 39 Mass pots of different plants together, to create a pleasant jungle effect in the corner of a small patio. The containers need not be large but the plants should be varied.

timber decked areas, balconies or roof gardens where you don't want the surface to be soaked, you will have to use matching saucers, drip trays or troughs.

One of the advantages of the container garden is that it is mobile and flexible, but large pots or tubs full of soil and plants can be heavy, so mount them on casters or small trolleys for mobility. The display can then be rearranged as required, individual specimens moved to a sunnier or shadier position as the days lengthen or shorten and tender plants can be moved under cover at the end of the summer.

# CHAPTER 2

# Plant Planning – Flowers and Foliage

You will find that even the most apparently careless profusion of plants has been thoughtfully planned if the arrangement is at all successful. The beauty of a container garden is that it offers complete control over colour, shape and form, with the added decorative dimension of the containers themselves. But that potential could result in disaster if you do not give some thought to style, harmony and pleasing contrasts within the final effect. Somehow, all the individual elements, the plants, the pots and their immediate surroundings, must come

*Fig 40   A beautiful arrangement in green and white using flowers and variegated foliage in a small terracotta bowl.*

together as a whole and produce an attractive three-dimensional picture that not only looks good on completion, but is designed to endure and improve, or at least maintain the same high standard, with maturity.

If this sounds like a tall order, especially for the amateur garden designer, do not despair. Container gardening is more a matter of fun than a chore; you can bite off as much as you feel you can chew at a time and, because it is so flexible, adjustments and alterations, or even a complete rethink are perfectly easy. Planning can be adapted to suit the time you have to spare and your own inclinations. People who enjoy playing around with statistics and planning down to the finest detail, might prefer to tackle the whole area in one go, working on a single theme such as colour or atmosphere to design anything from an all-white and green roof garden, to a Mediterranean-style patio. Those who find this prospect a bit daunting are better off taking an area at a time and building up the picture gradually. The important thing is to have a rough idea of how you want it to look when it is finished. Would you like a riot of colour through the year, a relaxing and subtle scheme of permanant foliage plants, an oriental atmosphere or the natural informality of a country cottage garden? Once that simple decision is made – and it may be dictated by the already established style of your home or the rest of the garden – it is surprising how the rest falls neatly into place. Even when planned and completed piecemeal, a style guide saves any

33

Fig 41    Fine architecture may demand a group of handsome containers like these magnificent urns planted in green and white.

hesitation over choosing individual elements and ensures they are going to be compatible. Thus you might restrict your plans to single pots or groups of containers at a time; so if you draw up a rough guide to where you are going to need a little height, the best place for something of special interest to catch the eye, which areas are damp and shady and which are hot, dry and sunny, and so on, you will know to which group of plants your selection will be restricted and avoid any practical mistakes without needing to prepare a major plan.

Generally speaking, whether planning a whole patio scheme or a single planter, you should be aiming for variety of height and breadth, good contrasting foliage shapes and sizes, and something of interest throughout the seasons, whether from a permanent display of evergreens or a succession of planting. Your final consideration will be colour and this is where container planning becomes the most fun, poring over the seed, bulb and plant catalogues as avidly as you would any pattern book or paint chart.

## VARIETY OF HEIGHT

An arrangement of plants in identical pots, growing to roughly the same height would look very dull and uninteresting, unless you are planning a particular formal effect like a pair of matching shrubs or trees to stand sentinel either side of a doorway or entrance; a collection of topiary, as equal as possible in size but featuring different shapes; or a row of identical shrubs or evergreen plants arranged to form a hedge or windbreak, or placed along either side of a path to create a temporary alley.

Informal arrangements need taller plants to the rear of the display, graduating to smaller, ground cover or trailing plants at the front, to soften the rim of the container and add a little width and body. Dwarf conifers and small, compact shrubs are useful for producing neat pyramid or bushy shapes at the rear of mixed planted containers planned for permanent display, with low-growing heathers, ivies or other trailers to the fore. Adopt a similar principle when planning your seasonal arrangements; the taller spring bulbs such as tulips and narcissi look more impressive rising out of a carpet of tiny forget-me-nots or dwarf wallflowers, than out of bare soil. Pots and window-boxes need a bright background of sturdy geraniums, carnations, African marigolds or petunias behind the creeping lobelias, alyssums and *Lysimachia*, the yellow flowered Creeping Jenny. With hanging baskets, plant your taller varieties to the centre of the container for the best, all-round effect.

Varying the height of plants within a container produces a good, solid display, but you will have to raise your sights if the overall scheme is to be successful. You can achieve some interesting effects simply by altering the height of your containers – useful where pots and planters only include a single specimen. Place classical urns and bowls on elegant pedestals to create an eye-catching focal point; raise pots on shelves or platforms; or use an old-fashioned, wrought iron style patio plant stand. Larger, taller containers can also play their part; a wide-bellied, narrow-necked urn could stand unplanted as an ornament among a collection of smaller, matching pots. The modern concrete planter ranges include a selection of taller styles for mixing shapes and heights.

There is also quite likely to be trellis, wind-breaks, screens or an ugly wall to brighten or disguise; sometimes, a trailing or climbing plant trained along an overhead pergola structure is important to provide some modicum of natural shade in an exposed roof garden or scorching sun-trap patio.

Larger shrubs and small trees are certainly

*Fig 42    Give some thought to how your pots are arranged; groups of three are always successful, especially when contrasting exotic foliage shapes.*

useful but often neglected container plants for paved areas – you should take care not to move large specimens too frequently, but since they are mobile, it may be a good opportunity to move them around occasionally to create an instantly different environment. More tender ornamental Mediterranean species can be overwintered indoors and brought out in summer to add a new dimension to your container scheme (*see* page 47).

To get right up on high, you are going to have to rely on climbers which should be kept well fed and watered, and can be trained on wires or trellis to soften side enclosures, or add flower or foliage interest at heights of up to 2·4–3m (8–10ft) depending on which plants you choose. A variegated foliage plant like gold-splashed ivy (*Hedera helix* 'Goldheart') or a pro-lific flowering climber like the beautiful *Clematis montana* could look stunning. Alternatively, devise an equally impressive but slightly more labour-intensive display using wall baskets, trellis-mounted pots and hanging baskets which can be attached to virtually any surface and at any height to show off your favourite combinations of plants. Remember to keep them within reach for watering though!

## VARIETY OF SHAPE AND TEXTURE

Planning for an attractive contrast of different plant and foliage shapes is more subtle and satis-fying than trying to balance too many colours. Both leaves and flowers offer many options of shape from daisy-like marguerites, pom pom marigolds and tiny star-shaped campanulas, to the wide and fascinating choice of variations among geraniums, ivies and ferns; or some of the more dramatic architectural plants such as bamboo, hostas and hardy palms. You should aim to combine a selection of tall, spiky or broad tongue-like shapes with the denser, lower-growing ovals, circles and pointed shapes; also look out for hearts and arrows, crowns,

35

Fig 43  Look out for interesting foliage contrasts or subtle harmonies in green.

Fig 44  Smaller plants can be grown in individual containers and grouped together.

hands, feathers and frills for a special position in your arrangement.

Remember that the shape of your plants also depends on their height and width. A mixture of a few formal, compact types with more sprawling, shaggy species is often highly successful. Dwarf conifers offer a huge choice of domes and pyramids, cones and prostrate forms. Alternatively, small-leaved evergreens such as box and privet can be clipped into classical topiary shapes. If you are looking for a formal topiary look but prefer a quick, inexpensive alternative, a fast-growing, small-leaved evergreen climber like ivy can be trained over a wire shape inserted firmly in the container. These are available in circular, domed and pyramid shapes; or devise your own designs using stout wire or treated timber.

Where plants are to be enjoyed at close quarters, it can be effective to contrast different textures. Plants offer a wide range of textures, from hard, shiny evergreen foliage, to the soft,

thick hairy leaves of many grey plants, the lustrous sheen of a lily, or the tousle-headed look of a French marigold. Thus an arrangement can be both visually stimulating and interesting to the touch – a point worth considering if any member of the household is visually handicapped, or for those who simply like to stroke or handle plants in passing.

## COLOUR

Within the range of leaves and flowers available for growing in containers, there are many colour combinations – sometimes within a single plant. There is also a huge choice of patterns including zonal geraniums with their distinctive marked foliage, striped petunias and spotted mimulus, or plants with marbled, banded or blotched leaves. The best results require a little self-control as too many contrasts can be confusing and unrelaxing. A profusion of

36

colour is fine in the summer hanging basket or tub, where the impression should be one of richness and variety. However, two or three bright colours balanced by plenty of green, or highlighted by white, is more than sufficient to create an attractive, balanced effect. A more limited colour scheme may have even more impact, for example, a green and white or green and yellow roof garden; a leafy patio restricted to green and cream foliage plants; a blaze of red tulips or carnations in a window-box. Sometimes a particular plant or new hybrid will suggest a design idea and with container gardening you can try out new schemes and ideas each season. These days, new varieties follow fashion trends with popular new shades and mixtures in both bright and pastel colours introduced each year. The biggest danger area to avoid is planting colours that clash too close together. For example, you should beware of

Fig 46 *A colour co-ordinated display can be as sophisticated as any interior accessory, as this arrangement of greens and golds illustrates.*

trying to combine different pinks and oranges – they rarely look good together and it is difficult to judge colours accurately from the seeds-men's catalogues or pictures on the plant packets. Instead of attempting to match a single colour, choose such close and pleasing harmonies as: blues and mauves, creams and yellows, reds and oranges, or pinks and purples, with an occasional contrasting or shocking shade for special impact in a selected spot. In this way you can build up a sophisticated and successful palette of colour effects. If you prefer to use a very limited range of shades, it is important to pay special attention to the variety of shape and size of leaves and flowers to maintain interest.

Fig 45 *A classic stone urn has suggested this sophisticated green and white theme.*

37

*Fig 47   Ornamental bowls on raised bases can brighten up a corner of the courtyard or garden.*

In choosing different combinations of shade and colour among your arrangement of container plants, it is easy to forget the impact and effect they may have within their immediate surroundings. Most pots and tubs, being of mainly natural materials like clay, stone and timber, are fairly neutral in tone, and look well against the majority of plants, unless, for example, you position a particularly hot shade of red or orange, or a strong blue or purple, against terracotta. You are more likely to lose impact by choosing plants too close in colour to your container – a silver foliaged scheme or white blooms will not have the same strong impact in a white painted wooden tub or concrete planter as they would displayed in contrast against natural timber or a russet pot.

Background can be equally important to the final effect, especially with window-boxes, wall baskets and other vertically mounted containers. Going for a strong contrast will show plants off to their best advantage and prevent them being camouflaged by their surroundings. Against red or similarly dark brickwork, avoid red and oranges and go instead for bright whites and soft blues, a touch of pale pink or something with silver foliage such as *Senecio maritima*. Grey stone needs deep strong colours such as purples, dark reds and golds. House walls are often painted white which presents the perfect opportunity to experiment with some of the strongest shades and hottest colours, avoiding any whites or creams which will not show up. Seaside properties are often painted pink or yellow, against which white and green look best, but there is also scope to experiment with reds and oranges.

Go for maximum impact with free-standing containers, avoiding a display of white blooms against a white painted trellis for example; or red flowers in front of a brown fence. Often the sheltering area behind will be clothed with a suitable climbing plant; in this case you will have to decide which takes priority at peak times of the year, as a curtain of pink or purple clematis or a mass of bright climbing roses could easily distract attention away from your pot arrangement, however carefully planned and planted.

## SCENT

Seating areas, entrances and passageways will be enhanced by the addition of scented plants. It is not a good idea to try to combine too many highly scented species – often one is sufficient at any given time of year, casting a single fragrance and not a heady and potentially unpleasant pot pourri. Plan for different plants to release their scent at various times of the year. You might enjoy the proximity of window-boxes or wall baskets of delicate snowdrops or *Chionodoxa* in spring – positioned nearer the nose for a time of year when you are unlikely to linger long in the garden. For summer, consider climbing honey-suckle, old-fashioned roses or sweet wisteria for the trellis, heady mock orange (*Philadelphus coronarius*) with its strongly fragranced white flowers, to be grown in elegant Versailles tubs,

or hanging baskets of spice- or fruit-scented geraniums. Do not forget scents for balmy summer evenings; some honeysuckles are evening scented, or grow tubs of night-scented stocks, and troughs of the new dwarf forms of the familiar tobacco plant. Herbs of course, perfect candidates for growing in tubs and pots, emit their blend of scents day and evening, after rain or under hot sunshine.

There are many plants with strongly scented foliage which are suitable for the container garden and will provide scents during the winter months. Tubs of clipped santolina, lavender and eucalyptus will all maintain a good display and release a strong, spicy scent if brushed against or rubbed between the fingertips. There are a surprising number of winter-flowering shrubs with a delightful fragrance, and if you are going to be using your container garden during the colder months, consider one of the scented viburnums, the useful dwarf evergreen sweet box (*Sarcococca*), or winter sweet (*Chimonanthus praecox*).

## INTEREST THROUGH THE SEASONS

Scent is not the only aspect of your container garden to be planned for all-year enjoyment. A strong background planting of trees, shrubs and evergreen foliage plants will ensure that your pots and tubs also look good most of the year; and to this you can add your favourite seasonal plants for extra impact and interest. Spring bulbs and annual bedding plants, selected for shape and colour, will allow you to experiment with new combinations every year and can be added to your existing containers or brought on under glass in separate pots to be added to the display as and when required. Your colour scheme may change only subtly through the seasons; or you may decide to ring the changes with a new combination of shades.

There is an equally fine choice available for autumn and winter displays of plant colour and

39

shape, so there is no excuse for the container garden to fade or die at the end of the year, which is important if the area constitutes the main view from the house. Tender varieties can be brought indoors to be replaced by pots and tubs of winter pansies or winter-flowering shrubs and ornamental evergreens. Hanging baskets can be replanted with different types of ivy and other hardy evergreen trailing plants if the walls look bare without their summer display, while sheltered window-boxes maintain a bright show through winter and early spring with snowdrops, cyclamen and primulas, violets, winter-flowering pansies and Christmas Pepper (*Capsicum annuum*) or the miniature cherry *Solanum capsicastrum*, both of which produce a dwarf bush of bright green leaves and brilliant red fruits.

Fig 48 Pots of sweet-scented spring bulbs can be brought on early and displayed on the balcony or terrace for extra interest.

# FOLIAGE EFFECTS

A good selection of foliage plants should form the background to your planting scheme, providing interesting shapes, a leafy green foil for bright seasonal flowers and, if you choose plenty of evergreens, winter interest. Maintenance is minimal, so you could convert the whole area to foliage grown in different containers to produce a lovely, relaxing, jungle-like atmosphere of greens, creams and greys. There is plenty of variety within leaf shape and colour, including variegated cultivars, to design an interesting and attractive display. Alternatively, use a selection of these more subtle shapes and colour combinations to offset the brightness of your blooms.

Many plants grown for their foliage have strong shapes and bold, architectural forms. Group them together to create arrangements of varying heights and contrasting leaf shapes, mix with flowering species, or plant particularly attractive specimens such as bamboo, fern or hosta in individual pots which can be added to your scheme or in key positions around the garden. They not only look good on the patio or terrace; you can stand them on either side of a doorway, on steps, or anywhere that needs a visual lift.

## Colours

We think of foliage plants as being green, but they encompass a colour spectrum almost as wide as that of flowers with their golds and silvers, creams, reds, pinks and purples. To extend the scope still further, variegated species, often hybridised for their ornamental effect, can be two or even three strongly contrasting shades in spots, stripes, borders and splashes. Variegated plants can sometimes revert to green, so any tendency to lose the colour markings should be cut out immediately to keep the plant true to form. Care must be taken not to combine too many different colours, and a strong coloured foliage not to have clashing

Fig 49 *A collection of foliage plants need not be evergreen but could encompass a selection of grey-leaved varieties.*

Fig 50 *Here a classical urn on a pedestal is planted with trailing green foliage plants for added effect.*

with your flowering plants or even with your containers. Foliage also offers textural contrasts from glossy green to woolly grey and these too can be used to pep up your scheme.

Silver, white or cream colours have a lovely lightening effect and silver *Cineraria* with its attractive curled leaves has long been a favourite for combining with brighter, flowering plants in containers. Other species may be edged or splashed with white, like *Fatsia japonica* 'Variegata', *Salvia officinalis* 'Tricolor' or *Ruta graveolens* 'Variegata'. *Hedera helix* 'Cavendishii' is a useful ivy with small mottled grey foliage, with every tiny leaf featuring cream edges. A useful 'evergreen' plant sometimes clipped into formal shapes is a variegated form of the common or English holly, *Ilex aquifolium* 'Argenteomarginata'. The junipers are a good source of leaves which are totally grey, white or cream with, among other, *Juniperus chinenis* 'Grey Owl', *J. scopulorum* 'Hill's Silver' and

*J.virginiana glauca* providing light relief. Similarly, use dwarf conifers to add silvers, greys and even quite strong blues to your scheme. *Abies concolor* 'Compacta' has bright silver-blue leaves, while *Chamaecyparis lawsoniana* 'Ellwood's Pillar' makes a narrow, feathery blue-grey pillar, and *Abies koreana* has dark green leaves with silver undersides and bright blue cones. For a softer effect, grow aromatic sun-loving plants reminiscent of the Mediterranean, like lavender, santolina or *Senecio greyii* – an excellent tough plant for windy sites such as roof gardens. Many saxifrages have silver or grey foliage and are excellent for creating a rock or alpine garden in a discarded sink, where a spread of houseleeks, *Sempervivum*, would also flourish, especially the variety *S. arach-noideum*, one of the palest.

Gold and yellow colouring adds a splash of sunshine to a scheme even when skies are grey. A gold and green theme can look stunning and

41

*Fig 51    Even small containers can support an interesting collection of foliage shapes.*

is easy to achieve with the many gold flowers and foliage available. For vertical interest, there is the beautiful scented honeysuckle, *Lonicera japonica* 'Aureoreticulata' with gold-veined leaves and white flowers which tend to turn yellow with age, or one of the many gold variegated ivies to be trained up walls and trellis screens, or allowed to cascade out of hanging baskets. One of the most popular is *Hedera helix* 'Goldheart' which has a central gold splash to each leaf, but the Persian ivy, *H. colchica* 'Dentata' is equally attractive with its large leaves and several yellow-marked varieties like 'Sulphur Heart' which is splashed with yellow, or 'Variegata' which has creamy yellow margins. There is a yellow cream-edged

periwinkle, *Vinca major* 'Variegata', which is particularly attractive, growing vigorously to make a bushy plant for special winter interest. Hostas can always be relied on for a dramatic display and there are several forms with bright golden yellow colouring. *Hosta fortunei* 'Albopicta' has oval leaves with yellow edges, while *H. f.* 'Aurea' is completely yellow.

Plants with distinctive red, blue and purple colouring can be used to add weight and impact to your scheme, but they must be chosen carefully or the overall effect can become top heavy. Choice of plant companions is important too; a specimen with strong blue foliage like *Picea mariana* 'Nana', which makes a compact ball perfect for small tubs and troughs, looks most attractive among grey and silver plants, but positioned next to dark green foliage or bright red, orange or yellow flowers, it would lose all its drama. Purple also looks good with silver, grey, blue and cream, and providing you don't introduce too many other shades, it can make a wonderful companion for pink. Red is a real eye-catcher – use it sparingly as a focal point, to add warmth to your display among white and green, or soften it with pinks and creams. You will have to wait until autumn for the majority of red and russet foliage effects when specimen Japanese maple, *Acer palmatum*, compact *Compressa thyoides* 'Rubicon' and climbing Virginia creeper, *Parthenocissus*, turn to flame. However, there are some plants whose young leaves do have a bronze or red tinge, while some like *Pieris* and *Photinia* are bright red. *Coleus blumei* offers a dazzling combination of colour variation.

If you are looking for blues, turn to the dwarf conifers. A great many have quite strong blue colouring including blue and white *Picea pumila* 'Dwarf Blue' and grey-blue *Picea sylvestris* 'Hybernica'. One of the most dramatic foliage plants with heart-shaped blue leaves and lilac flowers on purple stems is *Hosta* 'Halcyon'. For purple-red colouring, look out for plants with 'Purpurea' or 'Purpureum' in their name. The grapevine, *Vitis vinifera* 'Purpurea' has wine to purple coloured foliage. *Hedera helix* 'Chicago' has purple blotches on its leaves. Hybrid forms of *Phormium tenax* can also be relied on for some dramatic shapes and colours. 'Dark Delight' is black, 'Maori Chief' is red, and both have large blade-shaped leaves.

It is fun to experiment with different colour combinations but the real strength of foliage plants' design potential lies in the exciting variety of shape and size. You can contrast feathery ferns with the glossy, palmate False Castor-oil Plant, *Fatsia japonica*, or something tall and elegant like a bamboo with its tall canes and delicate fluttering leaves. Shapes range from tall, slender grasses, reeds and bamboos, to plants with spiky sword-shaped leaves like phormiums; from oval, heart and maple-shaped foliage of the ivies, to fleshy sempervivums, large, thick-leaved bergenias and pleated hostas. Styles range from the delicate *Acer palmatum* 'Dissectum' to the huge frilly head of an ornamental cabbage – a real eye-catcher in green-laced pink if grown in a series of small pots. Even within a single plant group there can be a fine choice of contrasts. For example, hardy ferns are among the most architectural and attractive plant ranges. *Matteuccia struthiopteris*, the Ostrich-feather Fern, makes a dense clump of familiar feathery fronds, but *Blechnum penna-marina* is low growing and makes more of a carpet of fronds, and the Hart's-tongue Fern, *Phyllitis scolopendrium*, produces flat, tongue-like evergreen foliage covered in brown spores.

A plant's very growth habit can also provide interesting contrasts, from the tall spiky types positioned at the rear of your arrangement, or centre if the container can be seen from all sides, to the creepers and trailers used to soften the edges of pots and tubs, smother walls and trellis or cascade out of hanging baskets. Trailing plants are both useful and adaptable. They might form a dense mat or cushion like the evergreen rock cresses, *Arabis*, which have hairy silver leaves and the many forms of thyme with tiny green or grey leaves, or the sunshine-loving *Helichrysum petiolatum*

which produces a curtain of silver heart-shaped leaves. Shady corners are well served by the trailing mass of soft yellow leaves produced by the golden form of Creeping Jenny, *Lysimachia nummularia* 'Aurea' – excellent for tubs, window-boxes or hanging baskets. Mother of Thousands, *Saxifraga stolonifera*, is also good for hanging baskets with its tiny plantlets of hairy round leaves on long thread-like stems – variety 'Tricolor' is particularly effective in red, green and white. Ivies are an obvious choice for shady areas and acaenas will also thrive, making an evergreen mat of silver, grey or bronze.

*Fig 52   Feathery ferns and palms look best in individual containers, which allows them to be displayed to best advantage.*

*Fig 53  You can't beat geraniums for vivid colour and plenty of blooms.*

## Geraniums for Foliage Interest

Geraniums, or *pelargoniums*, are understandably highly popular pot plants for tubs and containers, hanging baskets and window-boxes. Their blooms are bright and free-flowering, and with plenty of sunshine and no frost they can produce a succession of flowers for nine to ten months. They will grow almost anywhere, and can tolerate a considerable amount of neglect, surviving without watering for months. Prized for their vast range of reds and pinks (ranging from white through to purple, nearly black, some almost fluorescent in their brilliance), as much as for their toughness, it is easy to forget that pelargoniums also offer an excellent choice of decorative foliage options.

In fact, the leaf types have been extensively classified. Zonal geraniums for example, are a vast range, including thousands of cultivars with the familiar horseshoe markings in different combinations of shades of cream, green, purple

and burgundy, a highly attractive feature on a thick, felted leaf in a handsome frilled shape. Other forms are 'fancy leaved' pelargoniums, 'scented leaf' geraniums and dwarf, trailing and flowering types, many of which also come within the zonal group.

In a sunny position, the fancy leaved varieties will often produce flowers as well as stunning patterned foliage of red, green, yellow and brown. However, the leaf markings are more striking in a slightly shady tub or hanging basket and it may be worth sacrificing a mass of blooms for foliage interest. You will find a potash-biased feed will also strengthen the colours; avoid fertilisers with a high nitrogen content which tend to reduce the definition to almost nothing. If you are looking for shape as well as a wide range of colour variations, 'ivy-leaf' geraniums offer a couple of hundred varieties featuring pretty shaped leaves on trailing stems which can be trained up supports and over trellis, or can spill out of hanging baskets, troughs and wall pots. Many will also produce flowers, clustered at intervals along the main stems in shades of pink-white, lavender, magenta, red, salmon and pink.

There are other forms suitable for massed effects in hanging baskets and window-boxes, from the cascading 'Breakaway' series with an arching habit producing a mass of blooms in red or pink, to miniature and dwarf varieties perfect for edging small bowls and troughs and growing to a height of 8–23cm (3–9in). If you are looking for a more compact, bushy plant for window-boxes and troughs, there are the 'Deacons' and semi-double flowering 'Irenes'. Particularly attractive are the 'Stellar' geraniums with star-shaped foliage and single or double blooms; a perfect centrepiece for a tub or pot arrangement.

For tubs near sheltered seating areas or wall-mounted containers on a sunny wall or trellis, where plants may be brushed or touched, there are over 50 species of scented leaf geraniums, which have delicate, softly-shaded foliage and a delicious range of scents from lemon, orange and mint to spicy clove and verbena. Flowers tend to be insignificant, but the foliage is delightful and the scent a bonus.

Fig 54   In a sunny position geraniums will produce massed heads of flowers and a brilliant array of colours.

## Begonias for Flowers and Foliage

Good-natured begonias are a window-box and patio pot favourite, guaranteed to put on a brilliantly coloured display from summer through to the middle of autumn, looking good whether it rains or shines and even tolerating a certain amount of drought. There are a great many different hybrids offering a vast variety of colours and forms, from the simplest four-petalled flowers to extravagant frilled double blooms as lovely as any rose or camellia. They fall into three main groups, two of which are specially suited to being grown in containers, while the third is generally grown indoors where it will bloom all year round. This third type can often also be planted outdoors in summer.

Begonias with fibrous roots, which produce a mass of small waxy flowers in shades of red, pink and white, are excellent for patios and window-boxes and are easily grown from seed. Classified as *B. semperflorens*, they will continue blooming until the first frosts when a few plants removed to an indoor windowsill will last right through the winter. There are, in fact, some *winter* flowering begonias in this group known as 'Gloire de Lorraine'. Among the summer flowering fibrous rooted begonias, plants will grow to between 15–30cm (6–12in) depending on variety; and foliage colour varies from light and dark green to bronze or chocolate.

Tuberous rooted begonias form round, fleshy tubers which are normally placed, hollow side uppermost, in peat-based compost in late June. Generally called *B. x tuberhybrida*, the best-known type is *Grandiflora* which has particularly large and lovely blooms. Hybrids will flower from spring or early summer through to the start of winter, the crowded mass of double flowers each 5–6cm (2–2·5in) across in shades of red, pink, orange, apricot and yellow with a bright glossy green foliage. Some types are even more decorative, like 'Crispa Marginata' which has frilled, single flowers, or 'Marmorata' whose large double flowers are marbled,

*Fig 55    Red and white begonias show up well in a hanging basket set against an old grey and buff brick wall.*

edged and striped. As well as fringed and ruffled kinds, there are rose-like 'giant doubles' and the Pendula begonia whose trailing stems weighed down with large double flowers look superb in hanging baskets.

The third group is rhizomatous begonias which spread via a system of underground horizontal stems or rhizomes. This includes the popular *Begonia rex* hybrids, begonias whose spectacular heart-shaped foliage comes in a tremendous number of colour variations combining veins and markings, edges and blotches in bronze, green, red and silver. These are normally considered to be indoor plants, but they may well survive as part of a special summer display in a sheltered patio or balcony. *Begonia rex* plants are easily propagated from leaf cuttings.

## Propagation Tips

Begonias can be grown from seed, plantlings or tubers, depending on the type. The seed is very fine and should be sown in winter or early spring and kept moist until it germinates. Tubers are easier to grow, buried in trays of potting mixture in early spring and transferred to pots when several inches high. Large flowered types should be restricted to one or two shoots by pinching out, but allow several shoots with the trailing Pendula types. Many begonias can also be propagated successfully by cuttings. Stem cuttings are recommended for tuberous begonias

Begonias tolerate most potting composts and do not have any special requirements. However, where watering is concerned, a little

46

neglect is preferable to overwatering. You are well advised to let the compost get quite dry and then water by giving a good soaking, but do not allow the pot to remain standing in water.

## SITUATIONS

The damper, shadier areas of the garden, patio or backyard are often sadly neglected, for unless plants are chosen cautiously, the results will be disappointing and discouraging. Yet there are many species that will survive, especially in the protective environment of a container. Ferns and ivies will positively thrive, while other shade lovers have equally dramatic foliage. Lungwort, *Pulmonaria*, makes a dense clump of green leaves with white spots and Leopard's Bane, *Doronicum*, has heart-shaped leaves. A great many grasses and bamboos also prefer shady conditions: contrast these with fleshy hostas or clipped shapes of tiny-leaved box, or privet.

Patios, terraces and courtyards are positioned ideally to catch full sun and are often encouraged to become real sun-traps by painting the enclosing walls and fences white. The resulting light and heat is not always ideal for plants, but there are plenty that will flourish – Mediterranean species and even sub-tropical tender plants which can be brought under cover at the end of summer. It is important to choose plants that will tolerate hot dry conditions, otherwise you could find yourself watering two or three times a day. Many drought-tolerant plants have grey or fleshy foliage. Yarrow loves a hot sunny position and has silvery leaves, while hardy *Corydalis lutea* has fern-like foliage. There are a couple of ferns that will tolerate dry conditions if you are looking for foliage contrasts, such as the Deer's-foot Fern, *Davallia canariensis* and the Hart's-tongue Fern, *Phyllitis scolopendrium*. A collection of herbs would be perfect, mostly Mediterranean sun lovers with strong, coloured aromatic foliage which release their scent in the heat of the sun, like spiky rosemary, woolly

Fig 56 Highlight a shady corner with a lovely arum which enjoys damp, cool conditions.

grey sage, golden-leaved marjoram or one of the thymes with grey, green or purple-tinted foliage. If you are looking for an exotic touch, the area may be warm enough for a summer arrangement of bowls or troughs of cacti and succulents which can be brought indoors before the first frosts. Smaller species can be arranged in their pots on a bench, windowsill or table where they will be more easily seen and better appreciated.

If you fancy a little escapism, create a jungle-like atmosphere in your container garden with a selection of the more dramatic foliage species grown in large tubs or planters positioned close together where their bold leaves will make interesting contrasts. On a sun-trap patio or in a well-sheltered roof garden, half hardy plants may well survive, providing you offer some protection from frosts. You can reinforce the sub-tropical look with a few tender species that you bring indoors at the end of the summer, such as a large-leaved banana plant – *Musa paradisica* is the fruiting variety; *M. cavendishii* is a dwarf form – one of the spiky sago palms, *Cycas revoluta*, or an elegant date palm, *Phoenix canariensis*.

If you don't have the facilities for overwintering, or you feel that your container garden cannot offer quite enough warmth and sunshine required for more tender species, there is a surprising choice of exotic-looking but hardy

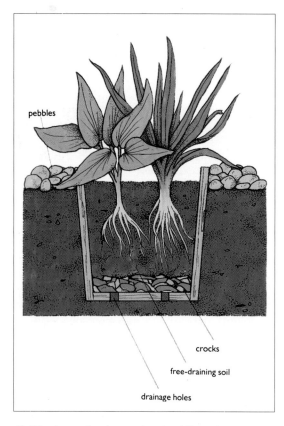

pebbles

crocks

free-draining soil

drainage holes

*Fig 57   A container bog garden. An old barrel or tub makes an excellent miniature bog garden, either stood in the shady corner of a patio or garden, or sunk into the ground and surrounded by pebbles. A couple of holes should be drilled in the bottom for drainage before filling with water saturated soil. Plant with moisture loving bog plants like iris, bog arum or hostas and keep the compost wet for an unusual display of dramatic foliage forms.*

plants which, if carefully selected and arranged, will produce a similar effect. The strong, spiky yucca, more familiar perhaps as a houseplant, is surprisingly tough, especially *Y. filamentosa* which often survives even a hard frost – providing it is given dry, sunny conditions in summer. Bamboos, with their coloured canes and fluttering leaves, are another group of hardy yet dramatic plants and are useful for adding slender height to an arrangement of more fleshy or dense feathery foliage. It is the palms that give a display that unmistakable air of an exotic jungle and there are several hardy species that make excellent pot or tub subjects. Moisture-loving *Phormium tenax* produces strong, sword-shaped leaves in a choice of colours including purple and the Chinese Fan Palm, *Trachycarpus fortunei*, is a classic, producing familiar fan-shaped sprays and growing to a height of 1·8–6m (6–20ft) in rich soil.

Some of the grasses would also be at home in an exotic setting and look spectacular grown in individual pots. *Miscanthus sacchariflorus* produces a dense mass of spiky green sword-shaped foliage, while *Festuca glauca* is smaller and spiky, growing to a dense cushion of glaucus blue to provide some interesting colour contrasts. For a complete contrast, the dramatic effect of the large, glossy, hand-shaped foliage of the False Castor-oil Plant, *Fatsia japonica*, is a garden designer's favourite which seems to flourish almost anywhere, with a lush appearance which belies its hardiness.

A sheltered spot, free from the worst frosts, extends your scope into the realms of the half hardy exotics which can remain outside protected by straw or sacking. You can create some stunning effects with frondy palms like the European Fan Palm, *Chamaerops humilis*, or the Cabbage Palm, *Cordyline australis*, which, unlike most other palms, will tolerate a poorer soil. For flowery interest, add a few exotic but easy-to-grow bulbs in separate pots. Try some of the loveliest lilies which are quite hardy, like the maroon or white *Lilium martagon*, giant *L. auratum*, with blooms up to 30cm (12in)

Fig 58   Shallow stone trays are perfect for creating miniature rock gardens where a collection of curious rosette-forming plants can be displayed on a bench or table to be more easily seen.

across, and golden Tiger Lilies, *L. tigrinum*. Plant the Scarborough Lily, *Vallota speciosa*, for early autumn interest. It likes to be a little pot-bound and will produce a mass of scarlet blooms on tall stems. More tender exotics like the Arum or Trumpet Lily – a wonderful combination of arrow-shaped leaves and large white trumpet blooms – and *Agapanthus umbellatus* (strap-shaped green leaves and huge flower heads on tall stems), can be grown indoors in tubs and brought outside in the summer.

## SEASONAL INTEREST

### Spring Cheer

There is nothing more cheering than the sight of the first spring bulbs coming into bloom early in the year. They are perfect for tubs and containers where they can provide a guaranteed succession of interest from Christmas right through to your first summer bedding plants, offering a huge variety of effects from the tiniest miniatures for sinks and troughs to the large and spectacular narcissi and tulips which make a colourful display in tubs, pots and window-boxes.

Most species can be planted out at the end of summer for the following spring, although some, like *Lilium candidum*, should be put into pots in midsummer, and others the previous spring. If your containers aren't clear of other plants, you could plant up your bulb display in separate pots or window-box liners and bring out when required, or force under glass in a cold-frame or greenhouse for a special early display. Crocus, hyacinths, daffodils, narcissi and double tulips are all good for forcing, if you select specially prepared bulbs and plant them

49

in containers of sandy potting mixture. Wrap them in black plastic or old newspaper and leave for eight to nine weeks. If you have no garden, a corner of the balcony or roof garden will do, unless you suffer really hard frosts, in which case bulbs will have to be stored indoors at a temperature of no more than 4°C (40°F). When the shoots begin to show, pots and bowls can be removed to the light. At the end of flowering, when the blooms have finished, bulbs should be lifted out and transferred to a spare bed in the garden or a tub of potting compost to die down and leave your containers free for the next season's planting. When the leaves have died, lift out the bulbs, clean them and store in a cool, dry place. Next year you can plant them out in the garden where they will, with luck, naturalise. For best results and to avoid disappointment, you should select new bulbs for your container display each year – this is a good opportunity to experiment with different combinations, new varieties and fresh colours.

The scope with bulbs is tremendous and everyone has their favourites. Save the standard, familiar forms of narcissi and tulip for massed displays in the garden and look out for something a little more unusual for your tub and window-box displays. They cost a little more, but small numbers go further in containers and the new colourings, double forms, frills and variations can be real eyecatchers. Narcissi, for example, are available with pink cups as well as gold; 'Salome' is particularly pretty. Alternatively, select one of the butterfly forms, sometimes called 'orchid flowering' narcissi and featuring an extraordinary frilled effect. 'Dolly Mollinger' has a curled crown of deep apricot against ivory petals, while 'Marie Jose' displays a stunning dark yellow star in the centre of each bloom.

Double flowered narcissi with their large blooms prefer a sheltered position. They feature a prominent frilled crown; charming apricot against white in the case of 'Petit Four', or creamy white on white for pretty 'Ice King'. The Cyclamineus narcissi are a dwarf form ideal for growing *en masse* in smaller tubs and in window-boxes. There are various coloured forms, all with swept back petals in shades of yellow, white and gold. Smaller still for delicate displays are the miniature narcissi like *N. asturiensis*, a tiny yellow trumpet daffodil which measures only 8–10cm (3–4in) tall; look out for the free-flowering 'Minnow' with its miniature lemon yellow blooms, and the extraordinary 'Rip Van Winkle' which has golden spiky flowers.

For a show of pure colour, you cannot beat tulips. They look best grown in groups of a single colour or closely matched shades, in tubs and planters, or troughs and window-boxes. Again, there is a very wide range of forms from tall stemmed varieties to frilled miniatures and a choice of flowering times enabling you to plan a continuous display from early spring through to early summer. Single and double early tulips which only grow to around 25–30cm (10–12in) are ideal for patio containers and window-boxes. Particularly recommended are the fragrant golden orange 'General de Wet', pure white 'Diana' and the double deep scarlet 'Carlton' (which, like many single and double tulips, is a good one for forcing).

Some of the later flowering tulips offer some beautiful variations that are worth considering as part of a late spring display. There are multi-flowered forms carrying up to six blooms on each stem, like the unusual burgundy brown and yellow 'Wallflower', and distinctive lily-flowered tulips, waisted with a pointed crown – try 'Marilyn', which looks like raspberry ripple ice-cream, with creamy white flowers streaked with red. Fringed tulips tend to be quite tall, although 'Fancy Frills' reaches only 41cm (16in), and makes a fine show of feathery edged blooms at the back of a spring arrangement. Similarly eye-catching are the Parrot tulips with their strong colour combinations (red and yellow streaks, dark purple, golden yellow, pink and green) and

*Fig 59 (opposite)   Some plants like the bog arum combine interesting leaves and flowers.*

*Fig 60   Japanese azaleas will provide a late spring display of pretty flowers.*

frilled petals, or the curious green streaked 'Viridiflora' types. There are various groups of dwarf, early flowering tulips like *kaufmanniana* and *greigii*, which are particularly good for window-boxes and patio containers, such as 'Johann Strauss' which combines dark red with gold and white, or the spotted foliage of 'Ann Salomons'.

Hyacinths seem specially designed for window-boxes and tubs, where bulbs should be planted in close groups about 10cm (4in) apart in a single colour or mixed shades of white, pink, purple, cream and blue. Excellent for pots and tubs are blue 'Ostara' and 'Pink Pearl'. Their tightly packed flower spikes and rich colours are attractive in themselves but, of course, hyacinths are particularly prized for their strong fragrance. They look especially good in a mixed arrangement with crocus or dwarf tulips in complementary strong colours to hide the base of the stems.

All the taller spring flowering bulbs benefit from the companionship of smaller flowering plants, or a handful of grass seed sprinkled on the top of the compost to produce a fine green carpet when the bulbs come into flower. Excellent companion plants, also ideal for alpine and miniature arrangements, are the grape hyacinths, *Muscari*, which will tolerate full sun or partial shade. The familiar tiny blue and purple fingers always look good below white and golden daffodils or narcissi, or blended with softer pink or peach tulips. Other forms available include the white scented *M. botryoides* 'Album', feathery violet *M. comosum* 'Plumosum', or the Feather Hyacinth, which produces tasselled blooms, and the wonderfully defined bright blue *M. azureum*.

Do look out for the more unusual crocus forms. They may be large flowered and pearly grey with lilac stripes like 'Pickwick' or a mass of smaller blooms flowering extremely early like 'Blue Bird', a stunning white with violet markings and golden centre, which is one of the *Crocus chrysanthus*. Other, more unusual forms include very early flowering *tommasinianus*, a species of crocus with silver grey and pale lavender markings. First herald of spring is the snowdrop, *Galanthus*, which in its common form *G. nivalis* can be planted anywhere in shade, under container-grown shrubs or taller flowering bulbs. More unusual, with larger flowers, coloured white with green tips is *G. n.* 'Viridapicis'.

Other delicate early spring flowers worth considering at the base of mixed planting arrangements, or used alone to create a beautiful miniature display, are *Chionodoxa*, Glory of the Snow, in shades of white, pink or bright blue, and pretty *Erythronium*, Dog's-tooth Violets, in pink, white and purple or hybrid form 'Pagoda' whose delicate yellow blooms and leaves have brown markings, and which thrives in shady conditions. 'Squills', or wild hyacinths are also well suited to spring planted outdoor containers, except perhaps the taller *Scilla cam-*

*panulata*, while *S. siberica* 'Spring Beauty' is perfect for pots and has bright blue flowers.

Spring companion plants need not be bulbs since there are also a great many low-growing, early flowering bi-annual species suitable for hiding the bases of taller plants and softening the edges of your container. Polyanthus flourish under most conditions and will bloom throughout a mild winter with bright green fleshy leaves and richly coloured blooms in a trough or window-box. As a partner to pink, purple or cream flowering tulips or pale lemon narcissi, a carpet of blue forget-me-nots, *Myosotis*, or early blooming, mat-forming saxifrage is ideal.

Spring flowering heathers are also useful for providing low carpets or spreading mats of dense colour early in the year as a companion to taller shrubs and trees in your permanent planters. There are many which come into their own in the spring and which prefer a lime-free compost making them excellent partners for other *Ericaceous* species like azaleas, rhododendrons and conifers. The tree heath, *Erica arborea*, produces fragrant white flowers and there is also a purple hybrid form. By contrast, *E. mediterranea* has tiny red flowers and is lime-tolerant. Hybrid forms include useful grey foliage and white flowers.

Three popular bi-annual spring bloomers with an attractive scent, and colour combinations which make them good container subjects, are the ubiquitous wallflower, *Cheiranthus cheiri*, in shades of russet, red, white, cream and yellow, Brompton stocks, *Matthiola*, producing flowery spikes of pink, red, white, yellow and purple, and Sweet William, *Dianthus barbatus*, with crimson, pink and white clusters of blooms. An attractive fragrance is a definite asset for spring and early summer tubs and baskets when the air is still fresh and the first sunshine of the year brings out the scent and a promise of good weather to come. Many of the bulbs already mentioned have a delicate scent; try to include some of the Poeticus narcissi, or the tiny Jonquilla forms, yellow tulip 'Bellona', or any of the hyacinths.

Do include spring flowering small shrubs and trees among your permanent planting, which can be planned to provide areas of special interest early in the season. The camellia, whose early flowers of white, pink or red show up well against the glossy leaves, is an excellent choice for a large planter in a shady corner where it can enjoy a rich lime-free soil. Remember that the blooms may need some protection against hard frosts. There are a great many beautiful rhododendrons including dwarf forms, whose late spring display of pinks, purples, white, yellow and burgundy and sturdy evergreen foliage can enhance a tub arrangement. Ornamental trees suitable for growing in a container, which have highly attractive spring blossom include the thorns, crab apples, cherries and rowans. *Sorbus* 'Joseph Rock'

*Fig 61    Adding pots of seasonal flowers will brighten up your display at high points of the year.*

offers good value in a limited setting with white spring blossom, good autumn colour and yellow berries. *Malus floribunda*, growing to only 3·6m (12ft), has pale pink blossom in spring and yellow berries in autumn, and popular *Crataegus oxyacantha* 'Paul's Scarlet' is distinguished by its bright red spring flowers.

Some patio climbers will also reward you with a curtain of blooms in spring and early summer, making a vertical display over walls or trellis. The heavy mauve or white, sweetly scented flower spikes of wisteria need to be well supported and can be trained across an overhead pergola structure to shade and protect a seating area. There are also spring flowering clematis, including the hardy evergreen *C. armandii*. With all tub-grown climbers, roots and stem should be well mulched to preserve moisture and protect from frosts.

## Summer Colour

Your pot-displayed trees and shrubs will invariably be looking at their best during the summer months and provide a good leafy framework, with perhaps the highlight of blossom or blooms as a focal point. They make a perfect basis on to which you can add a further layer of colour with the brilliant shades of free-flowering annuals which can be mixed and matched in tubs and pots, window-boxes and hanging baskets. You can be creative with both shape and colour, trying out new combinations and varieties – this freedom and scope is one of the best aspects of container gardening. Plants can be bought individually from your local nursery or garden centre, either fairly well advanced to fill up your containers quickly into the start of the season, or, more economically, if you get off to a sufficently early start, as small plantlings in 'strips' or blocks.

It is much better to grow your own varieties from seed though, and give yourself the pleasure of browsing through the seed catalogues and carousels. You will find a far superior range of shades for colour planning among the seeds,

and new introductions such as dwarf forms, double flowers and new fashion colours that a commercial grower will not take a risk with. You will have to do a little extra work and make an earlier start to the container gardening year to get propagation under way, and you will invariably end up with more plants than you need. Sell or exchange spares with fellow container gardeners, use them in the main garden or donate them to your local charity plant stall.

You may have a selection of perennial plants in pots that you have nursed through the

*Fig 62 Summer flowers are not all brash and bright: pretty daisy-like marguerites can be relied on for a delicate display, in a formal container.*

winter, perhaps a collection of begonias or geraniums, valued as much for their interesting foliage as their summer flowers. To these and to your overwintered greenery, add quick flowering annuals, or perennial border plants grown as annuals, producing results only a couple of months after sowing and, in most cases, providing a long and continuous display of blooms. Regular deadheading will keep your arrangements looking good and encourage plenty of new buds throughout the season. Plants will start to die back when flowering is finished, so remove quickly and replace with something new. In this way you can plan a series of different colourful effects throughout the season. Try to plan some kind of colour scheme and co-ordinate shades into complementary and contrasting groups to create the required atmosphere. Whites, creams, golds and yellows look lovely together and have a sunny or lightening effect, good for dingy backyards or dull balconies. Blues, mauves and purples are cool and sophisticated; you can warm them up with pink, lighten them with white or add a touch of red for a dramatic highlight. These are colour schemes to relax with – only plan for a real riot of contrasting colours like red and yellow, or bright blue and cerise pink, where a dull wall needs brightening or the area chosen can take such a strong effect.

Annuals may be added to your permanent plant display, or planted up separately in special pots, tubs and baskets. The advantage of this is that containers can be planned, planted and brought to a certain point of maturity before going on display, creating instant impact and enabling you to maintain a continuous, attractive show. This is particularly useful with hanging baskets which tend to look a little sad before the plants get going. It is also a good idea to completely change soil and liner at the beginning of the season. If you like to maintain something of interest all year round, it may be worth having separate 'winter baskets' of different trailing ivies and other evergreens which

can be lifted down and hung in a shadier spot until the end of summer. You can also use liners with window-boxes to ensure a continuous display.

Remember with all your planting schemes to vary height from the back or centre of the container towards the edges, using creepers, trailers and mat-forming varieties to spill over and soften the outline of the tub or pot. The majority of flowering plants prefer plenty of light and sunshine, but there are a few that will tolerate shadier conditions and still produce a show of blooms; save these for dark corners or a difficult location, or use shade tolerant evergreens in these spots.

Look out for compact and dwarf forms of familiar bedding plants to keep staking within your containers, and therefore maintenance, to a minimum. There are now low-growing varieties of antirrhinum, for example, which are compact and free-flowering and perfect for tubs or window-boxes. They tend to come in complementary mixed colours, like 'Pixie Mixed' which produces open petalled, butterfly-like blooms early in the season. An equally wide range of colours can be found among the nemesias which are quick and easy to grow producing a bushy plant covered in red, bronze, pink, orange, yellow or blue flowers. Excellent for hot, dry areas and tolerating a certain amount of neglect, is the brilliantly coloured nasturtium. Compact varieties like 'Whirlybird' are best for containers, growing to a height of only around 23cm (9in) and available in mixed shades of orange, red, russet and gold. The foliage is attractive too; a light green with cream marbling in the case of 'Alaska', while others, like 'Baby Salmon' and 'Empress of India' have dark tints.

If you are looking for a blaze of colour to brighten up a particular scheme, calceolarias are eye-catching, especially in window-boxes where they will flower for a long time, with their golden bubble-like blooms bright against the green foliage. Or choose marigolds, sturdy and free-flowering in a blaze of yellows and

Fig 63   A colourfully planted window-box highlights an almost hidden window.

golds, bronze and mahogany, above a dense mass of bright, feathery green foliage. African marigolds have the largest blooms and the 'Inca' varieties are low growing – to a height of around 25–28cm (10–11in) which makes them ideal for containers. The flowers are ball-shaped and free-blooming, unlikely to be damaged by bad weather, in glowing shades of orange and yellow. For smaller pots and window-boxes, dwarf French marigolds are always reliable, producing a continuous display of blooms throughout the summer given a sunny position and unspoiled by wind or rain. You can get both single and double flowering forms which grow to a height of around 13–15cm (5–6in) and present a vast range of interesting colour variations in stripes, borders and stars. Slightly taller at 23–25cm (9–10 in), are the Giant Crested types which feature large, early blooms with attractive curled and

frilled centres in apricot and mahogany, mahogany and red and orange colour combinations.

Equally attractive and frequently used for dramatic effect is *Salvia splendens*, producing fiery spikes of bright red above compact, dark green foliage. There are now other coloured forms in pink, purple and even white. *Salvia farinacea* 'Victoria' is blue and rather elegant, a perfect companion for a white flowering annual such as one of the new compact hybrid flowering tobaccos, *Nicotiana*, with its branching stems of attractive flowers. Nicotiana also comes in a choice of red, purple and pink shades – and a lime green, which is useful for subtle green and cream container combinations.

For a cottage-style patio or roof garden, why not combine roses and old-fashioned pinks, *dianthus*, in planters or tubs to make a delicate, sweetly scented display? There are a great many roses suitable for growing in containers if

56

you select the smaller-growing types like cream 'Alpine Sunset', golden 'Drambuie' or the popular pink *Floribunda* type 'Fleur Cowles'. There are also miniature roses which tend not to be scented but which only grow to around 20–30cm (8–12in) tall. 'Cinderella' is pink and 'Baby Masquerade' a lovely combination of gold and crimson. There are a couple of miniature climbers which could be trained over a decorative wire support firmly anchored in the container. Grow these with miniature pinks like 'Persian Carpet', a mass of small fringed flowers

in pinks, reds, salmon and white. Many *dianthus* hybrids will bloom early and continue flowering well into summer if you deadhead regularly. They include a beautiful range of plain and marbled pinks, whites and deep reds, massed among the spiky green or green and grey foliage and some have fringed flowers.

At the front of your pots and tubs or window-boxes you will need a close-growing edging plant like one of the mat-forming alpine types smothered in tiny but brightly coloured flowers. Cushion-like *alyssum* is a popular

*Fig 64   Roses are perennially popular, offering about 250 distinct species, many of which are ideal for growing in containers.*

choice, traditionally white, but now available in purple and lilac. 'Royal Carpet' is a scented variety, making a rich carpet of purple some 25cm (10in) across. Not making quite such a dense dome, but very pretty is *Anchusa* 'Blue Angel', a neat plant with long-lasting clusters of star-shaped blue flowers like giant forget-me-nots. Aubrieta, the Purple Rock Cress, is an evergreen with mauve or purple flowers, a good subject for sink gardens, as is soapwort, *Saponaria* with its mass of tiny pink or white flowers. For a dry, shady situation where you want to add a touch of lightness, Snow in Summer, *Cerastium tomentosum*, grows quickly and vigorously to form a close mat of silver-grey foliage and white flowers. Creepers and trailers are also useful for softening the outline of containers and providing up-front interest. Something like *Sedum sieboldii variegatum*, a creeper with delicate cream and blue or green foliage is very decorative, or grow an annual climber and allow it to trail – the Canary Creeper, *Tropaeolum canariense*, grows well and has pale green foliage with delicate fringed flowers of bright canary yellow. This could also be trained up a trellis or a free-standing support for a quick cover-up or vertical effect. Alternatively plant in hanging baskets and allow to trail in a curtain of elegant flowers and foliage.

There is an excellent choice of trailing or creeping plants with fine flowers that look good in hanging baskets or at the front of pots and window-boxes. Lobelia usually makes a neat dome of small blue flowers, a lovely spread of pure colour for a container arrangement, and

Fig 65  *Lobelia is a popular choice for hanging baskets because it forms a dense ball of tiny flowers and green foliage.*

Fig 66   An unusual but simple idea often makes the most eye-catching display, like these Saintpaulias grown in a hanging basket.

recently available also in white-eyed, all-white and red and white varieties, and 'Crystal Palace Compacta' with blue flowers against bronze foliage. Even better for hanging baskets are the Pendula or trailing types like the 'Cascade' series which produce a mass of tumbling colour, looking particularly effective in several shades of blue or a blend of light and dark blues, reds and lilacs. Basket campanula, *Campanula fragilis*, is another creeper with pretty blue or purple flowers on trailing stems; or for a curtain of soft light green leaves and golden flowers, choose Creeping Jenny, *Lysimachia nummularia*, which will thrive in a window-box or hanging basket in a shady position, or in a sunny position providing the soil is kept moist.

For a spectacular display, hybrid petunias guarantee vigorous growth and complete uniformity of colour and habit. The free-flowering, fairly compact single Multiflora types are perfect for large planters, pots and window-boxes growing to a height of around 30cm (12in) and blooming in bright pinks, blues and scarlets, with some varieties featuring clearly defined, white star-shaped markings. The Grandifloras have huge flowers and look very attractive in hanging baskets and window-boxes. Blooms can be as large as 11cm (4.5in) across in purple, pink, red or white, many of them bicoloured with veining or with contrasting star shapes. Equally popular are the hardy fuchsias with their exotic pendulous flowers in shades of pink, lilac, purple and white, and there is a whole range of varieties developed for growing as a cascade in hanging baskets and window-boxes. Alternatively, grow these in baskets on self-supporting poles to provide an area of eye-level interest on the patio or in the garden. They also look superb on either side of a path, framing an entrance or beside a seating area. There are also specially developed geraniums for hanging baskets, which will spill over the edges of containers. These cascading geraniums are from the 'ivy-leaf' group, so the foliage is particularly attractive, against which the delicate lilac, pink and orange flowers are displayed. You will need about three plants for a container 30cm (12in) in diameter, and in a window-box, set them approximately 20cm (8in) apart.

It is easy to find bright flowering plants for containers in sunny positions, but shadier sites need more careful planning, as pots and tubs in dark corners or small backyards can quickly look pale and spindly. Choose instead equally fine flowering but shade tolerating species like the delicate columbine, *Aquilegia*, which likes a cool and semi-shaded position, but will thrive in most locations. A compact form like 'Dragonfly' produces a mass of charming, nodding blooms, blending fresh blues, pinks, yellows and white. Another favourite for normally difficult cool, shady places is the magnificent Busy Lizzie, *Impatiens*, perfect for pots, baskets and window-boxes. Plants are compact and free-flowering, some producing blooms up to 5cm (2in) across in dazzling colour combinations.

Look for the miniature ground-hugging form, 'Novette', which produces a spread of large, glossy flowers in shades of orange, pink and red. Specially recommended for hanging baskets is 'Super Elfin Red' whose flowers are particularly bright.

The new hybrid Monkey Flowers, *Mimulus*, are extremely popular for window-boxes and hanging baskets, tolerating both sun and shade, providing the soil is kept moist. Plants are usually laden with the familiar strongly blotched flowers, which have been developed into fascinating colour combinations of orange, yellow, burgundy, brown and pink, against fresh green foliage.

## Autumn and Winter

A variety of plants can add interest to containers in winter, such as evergreen hellebores like *H. lividus* with its marbled leaves and green winter flowers, silver spotted lungwort, *Pulmonaria officinalis*, ferns and grasses, like *Phormium tenax*, which has some good hardy ornamental forms and alpines which can be grown as a collection in a separate planter or old sink. Grow hummock-forming *Polygala chamaebuxus* 'Grandiflora' with its glossy leaves and sometimes mild winter flowers, saxifrages, fleshy stonecrops, *Sedum*, and houseleeks, *Sempervivum*.

A selection of autumn flowering bulbs planted in large, mixed containers that can spare the permanent space, or cultivated in separate pots to be put on show when the foliage appears, can add their delicate blooms to your scheme after most summer flowering plants have finished. *Colchicum*, sometimes wrongly called the autumn crocus but more accurately, meadow saffron, has large white, mauve or purple flowers. Tiny *Colchicum autumnale* is first to flower and is followed by the larger *C. speciosum*. Both will tolerate a sunny or shady position and should be planted in mid-summer. There is also a pretty autumn daffodil, *Sternbergia lutea*, which blooms late in the season and looks more like a yellow crocus. It needs a well-drained, sheltered spot to flourish. Autumn flowering *Zephyranthes candida* must also have plenty of sunshine and does better in pots than in the garden in cooler climates. The foliage is like a green grassy mat above which the starry white flowers stand on long stems. For more dramatic effects and an unexpected touch of the exotic at the end of summer, there is a surprising number of bulbs with magnificent blooms suitable for pots in a prime position on the patio or positioned as the focal point of a formal garden. The more tender varieties can be brought on under glass and wintered inside after flowering. The Scarborough Lily, *Vallota speciosa*, prefers to be pot-bound, producing many bright scarlet trumpet-like flowers on tall stems. The pink or white trumpets of *Crinum x powellii* are large and scented, and pretty *Nerine bowdenii* can also be grown in pots outdoors in a sunny position and produces umbels of lily-like flowers. Winter blooming dwarf cyclamen with their delicate, butterfly-like flowers standing above the fleshy foliage on coloured stems, are an unexpected sight in winter, perfect for pots where they are more easily seen and appreciated. *C. x atkinsii* has deep pink flowers and large leaves with silver markings. Other species may have white or paler pink flowers.

# CHAPTER 3

# Plant Planning – Trees, Shrubs and Edibles

## TREES AND SHRUBS

Many of the smaller trees and shrubs are excellent subjects for growing in containers where, providing they are adequately fed and watered, they will flourish, the size of the container limiting the mature size of the specimen to even more suitable proportions. Alternatively, you could create standard and half standard formal trees with a mop-head of foliage on a long tall stem using grafting techniques and decorative shrubs such as broom, or *Salix helvetica* with its grey-green foliage and spring catkins. Both formal and informal trees and shrubs are a valuable addition to your scheme, producing a fuller, more mature effect on the patio or roof garden where height and breadth is important. Many hybrid trees and shrubs also

*Fig 67  Arrange formal topiary shapes in groups or rows along paths or around the boundaries of a patio or roof garden.*

Fig 68 *Ornamental shapes. Small leaved evergreens can be trained and clipped into ornamental shapes: box (*Buxus*), privet (*Ligustrum*) and yew (*Taxus*) are the best species for topiary. Many shrubby and sub-shrubby plants like geraniums and fuchsias can be grown as a standard by special pruning techniques.*

*Laurus nobilis*, honeysuckle, *Lonicera*, or blue hibiscus, smothered in exotic, large blue flowers with a dark maroon 'eye' from summer into autumn. A standard marguerite covered in large daisy-like flowers makes a fine, decorative specimen for 'outdoor rooms' or positioned on either side of a formal door. Pruning and training involves cutting off the lower lateral shoots as they appear on pot-grown plants, leaving the lower stem exposed. Alternatively, the plant can be grafted on to the stem. You will need to support the plant with a cane and encourage the top to bush out by also removing any lateral shoots at the top of the stem, cutting just above the new buds. This produces a dense mass of flowers and foliage on top of a long straight stem. Tender varieties can be brought under cover at the onset of winter.

## Choice

Your choice of shrubs and small trees will be limited by the space available and the need for something to provide spring, summer, autumn or all-year interest. Almost any slow-growing or dwarf shrub or tree can be grown in a container, providing you give it such attention as watering and spraying the foliage in hot weather, which is particularly important for conifers and evergreens, pruning, shading and, in the event of a bad winter, moving under cover or packing the container with straw or sacking to prevent it freezing.

There is a huge range of dwarf conifers, virtually all of which are perfect pot plants, but which tend to look better grown in architecural groups of different heights and textures than dotted about on their own looking lonely. The best way to display individual specimens such as a compact and naturally shapely form like *Juniperus communis* 'Compressa' or *Chamaecyparis lawsoniana* 'Green Globe', is to plant them on either side of a doorway or entrance. Dwarf conifers are generally grown for their wonderful variety of shape and texture, embracing dark and light greens, gold, silver, bronze or blue in

offer excellent ornamental value; bred to be smaller or more compact, they will often provide something of interest in spring and autumn as well as summer, so will add more than just height to your scheme. Trees are useful for shade and shelter, and to protect other plants.

Trees and shrubs can also be trained into formal or ornamental shapes ideal for displaying in a pot or planter. Evergreen hedging plants like box, *Buxus sempervirens*, and privet, *Ligustrum ovalifolium*, may be clipped into geometric shapes such as spheres, pyramids and columns which are particularly suited to pairing up in pots on either side of a seat, steps or doorway. The shrub will need clipping three or four times a year to produce the initial shape. Other suitable plants for clipping include holly, *Ilex aquifolium*, yew, *Taxus baccata*, or cotton lavender, *Santolina*, in green or grey. Other trees or shrubs which can be successfully grown as mop-head standards include the lovely rose, *Rosa*, bay, close-growing domes and pyramids or rambling prostrate forms. *Thuja occidentalis* 'Danica', for example, makes a neat ball of dark green in summer and bronze in winter; *Juniperus chinensis* 'Pyramidalis' grows to make a pyramid of silver blue.

The Japanese maples are a group worth exploring for a wide choice of small, ornamental trees that can offer good value and often all-year interest. All *Acer palmatum* are slow growing and will tolerate a shady position, although they do prefer a little sunshine. There are many forms, with different colourings and leaf types; *A. p.* 'Aureum' for example, has yellow leaves which turn golden later in the year, while *A. p.* 'Atropurpureum' has bright red leaves. Especially suitable for containers is *A. p.* 'Dissectum' which is barely more than a shrub reaching only 3m (10ft) at maturity. The foliage is deeply cut to the extent of being feathery and there is also an eye-catching purple form.

Choose deciduous trees like this with good autumn colour as well as summer interest and

*Fig 69   A flowering evergreen shrub and trellis make perfect screening on a windy roof garden. Note the lightweight timber decking.*

you are really getting your money's worth. Other specimens of good value include the crab apples, *Malus*, which produce scented spring blossoms; some have colourful fruits and also have attractively coloured foliage in autumn. One of the smallest is *Malus* 'Red Jade' which has an attractive pendulous habit. The flowering cherry, *Prunus*, is another compact and highly decorative large group of hybrids. *Prunus* 'Accolade' opens a solid mass of semi-double pink blossoms in the spring, while *P.* 'Amanogawa' is a Japanese cherry, specially developed for its upright habit – useful where space is restricted – with scented pink flowers in spring, later displaying small black fruits and yellow tinted young foliage.

The rowan, *Sorbus*, is a handsome tree with slender green foliage, turning to fire in autumn, and producing interesting berries. The American mountain ash, *Sorbus americana*, does well in an acidic compost and has white flowers, delicate leaves and round red fruits that usually decorate the bare branches all winter. *Robinia* is fast growing, making a canopy of fern-like leaves and pretty, sometimes scented flowers in summer. *R. pseudacacia*, the false acacia tree, has a popular golden form 'Frisia'. For restricted space and a dry sunny situation, grow *R. p.* 'Pyramidalis' which makes a neat column. *R. p.* 'Umbraculifera', also known as the Mop-head Acacia, is slow growing and makes a round, compact head of foliage.

The hawthorn, *Crataegus*, grown as a small tree, can make a fine display for most of the year with spring blossom, interesting fruits and autumn tints. There are many forms of this small tree, including *C. oxyacantha* 'Aurea', which usually has glossy green foliage, white flowers and yellow fruits; but the variety 'Paul's Scarlet' has wonderful red double flowers. Azaleas and rhododendrons are often well suited to a leafy container garden since they will not tolerate any lime in the soil and can be supplied with a good acid compost. There are a great many forms including dwarf hybrids, but all provide highly attractive, glossy evergreen

*Fig 70* Hydrangea macrophylla *is perfect for growing in tubs, and its small star-shaped flowers have a long season.*

leaves and spectacular, exotic blooms in shades of red, pink and purple or sometimes yellow, white or gold. They prefer light shade and plenty of moisture. Another beautiful flowering shrub that will tolerate shade and prefers a lime-free soil is the camellia in either spring or winter flowering species.

*Hydrangea macrophylla* is frequently seen in tubs with its giant white, pink, red or blue blooms remaining on the plant for months. If you are looking for a hardy shrub with a strong spring fragrance, lilac, *Syringa vulgaris*, does best in a sunny position and comes in a choice of hybrid forms with single or double flowers in a range of colours. There is a dwarf form for tubs, growing to a height of only 1·5m (5ft) and

sweetly scented. For the front of the house or a roof garden, you will need a hardy tree or shrub with a reasonable resistance to pollution such as golden foliaged Scotch Laburnum, *Laburnum alpinum*, which has shiny leaves and large flower clusters.

Other shrubs which offer scent as well as colour include *Skimmia japonica*, a low-growing evergreen with fragrant white flowers, which grows only to around 1m (3ft) in a tub, or oleander, *Nerium oleander*, a fine tub display of red, pink or white flowers in summer, which like bay, *Laurus nobilis*, citrus and other more tender species, can be moved under cover and overwintered without fear of frost at the end of the season. Hardier, but no less beautiful, are roses, which are perfect for all kinds of pots and containers, whether grown as a standard tree, the blooms massed on top of a slender stem, as a bush or as a climber, trained over a shaped support or up a trellis. Small weeping trees and shrubs can look very attractive as the focal point of a container-planted patio or garden. The weeping birch, *Betula pendula* 'Youngii' grows only to 3m (10ft) high, its feathery foliage reaching right down to the ground and there is also an eye-catching purple form of the weeping beech, *Fagus sylvatica* 'Purpurea Pendula' which is worth considering.

*Fig 71 A glossy evergreen with handsome shaped leaves like* Fatsia japonica *makes an excellent foliage plant for individual containers.*

Other dwarf or compact decorative ideas for focal points include the Pea Tree, *Caragna arborescens* 'Pendula' with fine feathery foliage and a mass of attractive yellow pea-like blooms grafted on to a 1.2m (4ft) stem, a Pagoda Bush, *Enkianthus integra* 'Hakuronishiki', a dwarf willow with silver variegated foliage, weeping cotoneasters or Blue Holly grown as half standards or *Cytisus* 'White Bouquet', a compact dwarf form with cascading branches of strongly scented blooms which is ideal for pots and tubs.

Some shrubs and grasses are valuable for your planned scheme, individually planted in tubs and pots and specially chosen for their dramatic or architectural appearance. Bamboo looks very exotic with its tall slender canes in a variety of colours and fluttering oriental-style foliage and Pampas Grass, *Cortaderia selloana*, produces equally elegant feathery plumes. By complete contrast, the False Castor-oil palm, *Fatsia japonica*, has large, glossy evergreen leaves shaped like hands and thrives on sunshine. The common fig, *Ficus carica*, is equally handsome and sun-loving; a fast-growing tree, it produces wide shady branches and restricting its roots in a pot encourages it to fruit which could happen at any time after four years.

## Situations

For roof gardens and windy balconies, the lower growing shrubs will stand up to exposure to strong winds, cold winter temperatures and unrelieved summer heat much better than taller species. More compact bushes include the daphnes which, providing they have a rich soil, good drainage and plenty of moisture, will make a highly attractive shrub with fragrant flowers. Useful for shade is the Rose of Sharon, *Hypericum calycinum*, which will be smothered in tiny flowers in summer.

Others prefer plenty of sunshine but are tough enough to survive hot dry conditions and a certain amount of neglect. Bringing tubs under cover or covering with straw or another suitable insulating material, helps them survive a cold winter. *Eucalyptus gunii* is useful for its silver foliage colour and is reasonably hardy although it may be killed by prolonged frost. *Cistus* also tends to be a little tender but is a useful evergreen with aromatic foliage and flowers rather like a rose which gives it its common name of Rock Rose.

Hardy, but enjoying plenty of sunshine are the shrubby potentillas, *Potentilla fruticosa*, with their tiny leaves and a mass of white or yellow flowers in summer. Handsome *Aucuba japonica* is a robust-looking plant with large glossy green leaves sometimes splashed with yellow and bright red berries. Southernwood, *Artemisia abrotanum*, is another fragrant evergreen which likes to be positioned in full sunshine.

Some more tender species of flowering shrubs can be grown in a conservatory or similar cool but light indoor plant environment, and stood outside during the warmer, summer months. The Bottle-brush, *Callistemon citrinus*, produces startling red bristly blooms, like giant brushes, *Abelia grandiflora* has pink or white summer flowers, the Coffee plant, *Coffea arabica*, displays white spring flowers against the shiny evergreen foliage and later, in summer, red berries. If you can provide warmth in winter, the range can be extended to free-flowering *Lagerstroemia speciosa* with its purple flowers right through summer, or pretty *Jacaranda acutifolia* which has blue blooms.

Climbing shrubs are invaluable for providing vertical interest, or for disguising or decorating trellis, tall walls and other surrounding screens with flowers and foliage, and sometimes fruit. Eye-catchers for sunny positions include climbing roses and hardy jasmine with its delicate scented flowers. *Jasminum officinale* blooms in mid-summer, while yellow flowered *J. nudiflorum* blooms in winter. Both will do well in pots. Some climbers like their flowers to be in sunshine, but prefer their roots in shade, so tubs and planters should be well mulched or covered with a layer of moisture-retaining pebbles before standing in a shady spot. This includes the

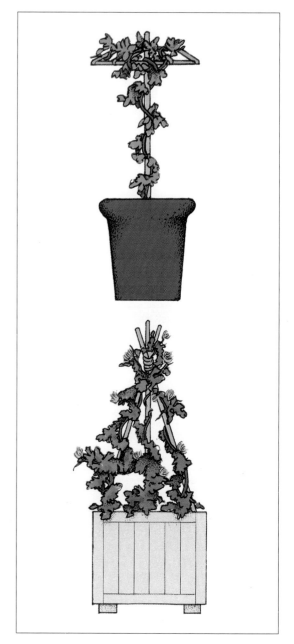

*Fig 72   Supports for climbing plants. Quick climbers like honeysuckle or jasmine can be grown into a standard by training two stems up a pole and round a wire frame; or a leafy climber like ivy or hops can be grown up a wigwam of poles.*

Fig 73   A climbing rose makes a fabulous display on the house wall or boundary fence and the smaller, less vigorous varieties are perfect for containers.

honeysuckle, *Lonicera*, guaranteed to conjure up a country atmosphere with both evergreen and deciduous types, day- and night-scented flowers and a completely shade-tolerant gold variegated variety 'Aureoreticulata', and clematis, again offering both evergreen and deciduous kinds and a wide choice of spring, summer and autumn flowering varieties, with a great many lovely flower forms.

For an exotic touch, a Passion Flower, *Passiflora caerulea* will often survive the winter, or try a stunning trumpet vine, *Tecoma radicans* with its giant clusters of bright flowers and the vigorous potato vine, *Solanum crispum*, in a sheltered position. Another good climber for

quick results is *Polygonum baldschuanicum* which can grow as much as 4·5m (15ft) in a season and produces pretty flowers in late summer in a sunny position.

Shady backyards can take full advantage of the huge range of different coloured and patterned ivies, *Hedera*, or deciduous *Hydrangea anomala petiolaris* which has the added bonus of huge white flower heads in summer. Annual climbers can be useful for a temporary display to be changed for a new look every year. Nasturtiums, *Tropaeolum majus*, provide brilliant colour; bright orange and yellow flowers against large, light green foliage, and will tolerate some shade. On the other hand, Morning Glory, *Ipomoea purpurea*, needs full sun and a sheltered position for its red, pink, purple, blue and white flowers to flourish. Canary creeper, *Tropaeolum peregrinum*, also makes a good display with its delicate, feathery leaves and tasselled yellow flowers.

## Autumn and Winter Interest

The container garden is invariably an extension of the home, a kind of outdoor living room, often, in the case of a patio, balcony and sometimes a roof garden, opening out from one of the rooms themselves. It is an area you will wish to use all year round, or at least, to look good through the seasons. This is particularly important where the area is visible from the house since it frequently forms a kind of living picture or panorama from the living room, dining room or kitchen.

Conscientious deadheading and plant replacement as a matter of routine tidiness will keep your containers looking in top condition for as long as possible. However, there comes a day, when summer is on the wane and the weather is starting to cool, when the majority of summer flowering plants are finishing, and your display starts thinning out. There is a surprisingly wide variety of interesting plants to choose from that peak towards the end of the year with fine foliage or flowering effects for autumn, but they

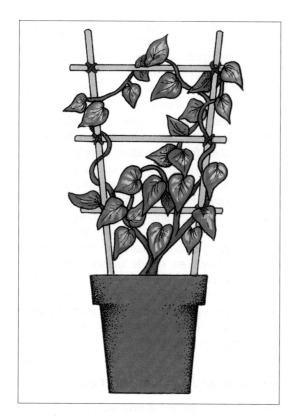

*Fig 74    A free-standing trellis made of bamboo or split cane enables climbing plants like ivies or vines to be grown in containers.*

There are the rich autumn tints of some of the smaller deciduous trees whose foliage may turn gold, bronze, russet or even scarlet; shrubs which bloom in the colder months, frequently with beautifully scented flowers to impart a fragrance that is sharpened by the crisper autumn air; autumn flowering bulbs; and even climbers which can be used to keep trellis, walls and other vertical surfaces in focus during the duller months. All can be used to good effect in your pots and tubs, producing either a blaze of mingled hot colours before the more austere winter display of predominantly glossy ever-green foliage, white flowers and red berries, or positioned among a permanent planting arrangement to provide areas of special interest or colourful highlights. Some shrubs and trees are so versatile that they can offer something of interest right through the year with spring blossom, fine summer foliage, autumn fruits or berries and colourful leaves, plus good bark colour and a handsome skele-ton during the winter. These plants offer excel-lent value for small patios or gardens where space is limited and it is worth taking them as the starting point of your container scheme and planning other features round them.

If you want your container garden to main-tain a good, basic permanent design, matured to the required 'shape' and style, to which you add seasonal highlights like spring bulbs and summer annuals, a collection of varied ever-greens will look good whatever the time of year. They cover such a huge range of forms, shapes and colours from climbers, shrubs, trees and perennials to shades from evergreen to blue, grey, bronze, silver, russet and scarlet, that there is plenty of scope for creative design and exciting effects. Many evergreen plants also produce fine flowers or berries, making it possible, with mulching and automatic watering systems, to devise a virtually no-maintenance garden that does away with seasonal planting out and cutting back.

For a permanent vertical screen, important where privacy or shelter is a priority, ivies are

need to be carefully chosen and positioned, as a continuation of your overall scheme, so that you do not have any gaps or awkward over-laps. One solution is to grow the majority of autumn interest specimens in separate contain-ers and bring them into play when required, but a selection of permanent features – a shrub or tree perhaps – might integrate very well into your main display and create a balanced, mature effect. The important thing is to plan for it. It is easy in the rush of enthusiasm for all those fine colourful summer flowers and spring bulbs, to forget the latter part of the year, but equal care in planning something of interest during winter and autumn will be well rewarded by an area that gives you pleasure every day of the year for very little extra effort.

Fig 75    Some bright flowering plants will
flourish in pots in semi-shade, like pretty
primulas.

Fig 76    For autumn colour the foliage of
Euonymus is invaluable; above are three types,
including E. fortunei 'Silver Queen'.

an obvious choice with their pretty-shaped leaves and choice of patterns and colours. One of the finest is the Persian ivy, *Hedera colchica dentata*, which has large, glossy heart-shaped leaves. If you require a more colourful effect, choose one of the variegated varieties of *Hedera helix* with gold, silver, cream or white markings. The self-clinging *Trachelospermum majus* makes an attractive curtain of elliptic foliage, some of which turns red in winter.

Several familiar flowering climbers have evergreen forms if you are looking for a permanent leafy display as well as a curtain of summer blooms, for example, vigorous honeysuckle, *Lonicera japonica* is an evergreen with highly scented white flowers, which turn to yellow. Varieties *L. j.* 'Aureoreticulata' with gold veining on the leaves and *L. j.* 'Halliana' which has bright green leaves on purple stems, are

particularly eye-catching and although a little more tender than the original, will only lose a few leaves in a hard winter. Evergreen clematis tend to have smaller, more modest flowers than their showy deciduous cousins, but they are equally beautiful. *C. cirrhosa* has deeply cut, fern-like foliage on slender stems which can have a most attractive bronze-purple tint. The creamy flowers are bell-shaped and appear from winter to early spring unless the weather is exceptionally cold. Very popular is *C. armandii* whose leaves are up to 15cm (6in) long and rather leathery. The spring flowers are white or cream, later taking on a pink tinge depending on the hybrid. Do not forget that some roses have evergreen or semi-evergreen leaves, particularly if the position is sheltered. If you are lucky 'Madame Gregoire Staechelin' will hold on to the majority of its leaves through winter after producing a magnificent display of climbing blooms in summer.

Sometimes it can be more advantageous to use a deciduous climber to allow a little extra light on to the area in winter after the leaves have fallen, especially where the climber or creeper has been trained across an overhead pergola structure to provide welcome shade from hot sunshine in summer. Some climbers can offer something of interest in autumn or winter instead of a show of leaves. Hardy *Ceratostigma plumbaginoides* dies back in a blaze of glory when the leaves turn bright red at the end of summer, while *Jasminum nudiflorum* covers its naked stems with delightful yellow flowers in winter.

Trees and shrubs can offer a wide and exciting range of permanent effects for your tubs and containers. These include not only dwarf conifers with their formal domes and pyramids, or spreading mounds of blue, grey, green, gold and bronze (some produce special winter colouring – like domed *Chamaecyparis lawsoniana* 'Aurea Densa' which turns gold and *Thuja occidentalis* 'Rheingold' which changes to bright copper in winter), but also small-leaved evergreens like box, privet and yew for clipping into topiary forms; interesting small evergreens like the bay laurel, *Laurus nobilis*, the Silk Tassel Tree, *Garrya elliptica*, which features glossy green leaves and silvery catkins; and all the fine shrubs from grey sages, *Salvia*, tiny-leaved broom, *Ruscus*, and dramatic *Fatsia japonica* with its large, glossy leaves, to elegant, oriental bamboos like *Phyllostachys aureosulcata* which has yellow canes, *Arundinaria nitida* with purple markings and *A. viridistrata* – a clump of stems with green and yellow stripes.

Fig 77  A collection of evergreens cut into formal shapes make an interesting permanent feature in pots on the patio or balcony.

Fig 78  Small-leaved evergreens can be clipped into domes and spirals.

You will find that many of the evergreen shrubs offer the bonus of beautiful flowers or bright berries at certain times of the year, as well as a permanent display of fine foliage. Holly is an obvious example with its wider range of coloured foliage patterns and different kinds of berry options. *Skimmia japonica* also has excellent red berries, *Daphne odora* produces deliciously scented white flowers in winter and the viburnums often combine handsome foliage with fragrant white flowers and blue-black fruits. The evergreen daisy bushes, *Olearia*, are also justifiably popular with their rounded habit, the bush covered in leathery leaves and tiny white, often scented, daisy-like flowers. There are many winter and autumn flowering heaths and heathers which can make a dense carpet of colour at the base of a taller or long-stemmed plant in a large planter or pot or be combined in a single container. *Calluna vulgaris* 'Blaze-away' has mauve flowers in autumn and red foliage in winter, lime-tolerant *Erica carnea* is winter flowering, with varieties including excellent colour combinations such as 'Foxhollow' which has pale pink flowers and yellow foliage with a red tinge in winter, or 'Adrienne Duncan' which has red flowers against bronze foliage.

Other plants which can be relied on for a special autumn or winter display include small deciduous trees like sorbus, malus and the glorious Japanese maples, *Acer palmatum*, whose foliage turns magnificent shades of red, gold, yellow or bronze, shrubs like *Hamamelis* × *intermedia* 'Jelena'; or the shrubby dogwoods, *Cornus*, some of which have brightly coloured stems in winter – *C. alba* has bright red stems with the bonus of white flowers in spring and *C. a.* 'Spaethii' is a yellow variety with red winter bark. *Prunus subhirtella* 'Autumnalis' is a handsome flowering cherry which blooms in autumn. Some of the later summer flowering plants may also last well into autumn and beyond if the frosts hold off, maintaining a colourful display of blooms. These include dahlias (the anemone-flowered types are particularly good for tubs) and asters, particularly

*Fig 79*   Acer palmatum *'Dissectum' (Japanese Maple) is slow growing but has excellent foliage.*

the low-growing types, which can be bought in individual colours such as blue, pink, red or white for special design effects.

## EDIBLES

For those with only a patio, balcony or terrace and no garden, certain fruits and vegetables can be successfully grown in containers, hanging baskets and window-boxes. If you already have an adequate vegetable patch, a sheltered patio area or small balcony which receives plenty of sunshine can also offer the chance to grow a few more tender varieties and get them to ripen quickly without a greenhouse. Tomatoes, sweet peppers, courgettes and aubergines would all benefit from being grown in a large container of rich compost or a commercial grow-bag in a sunny spot.

If your garden is very small, it may be worth creating a complete vegetable or fruit garden in pots and tubs, to stand on paving slabs, timber-decked areas or low platforms to receive maximum light and warmth. There will be no need to rotate crops, no heavy digging, no weeding and no build-up of pests and disease in the soil as fresh compost could be used for each new crop. Soil can be exactly geared to the plant's needs, from sandy and free-draining for tiny 'Rondo' carrots, to a richer soil for a greedy crop such as tomatoes or beans. Since your vegetable plot is completely mobile, you can move it around as required to get sufficient light and sun. By selecting compact, dwarf yet high yielding varieties, the container-sized fruit or vegetable garden should be sufficient for the needs of a small family and, should you require more, then simply plant up another container!

The only disadvantage of growing edible plants in a limited space is that containers will need very careful feeding and watering if they are not to become deficient, but since this is part of the regular care routine of an ordinary kitchen garden, it should not involve a huge amount of extra work. A well-organised container garden for edibles may well lend itself to an automatic feeding and watering system and mulching any areas of bare soil with straw, bark chips or pebbles will help cut down moisture loss and keep weeds at bay. Some edible plants lend themselves to a certain type of container; for example strawberries in special pocketed strawberry barrels or tubs; cherry tomato plants with their trailing stems in hanging

Fig 80   Growing your fruit garden in containers is the perfect opportunity to experiment with early crops or more tender varieties, that can be moved to a more sheltered or heated position as required, like strawberries, grapes and citrus fruits.

*Fig 81   An attractive, and edible display of parsley, grown in a shallow trough and mulched with pebbles to conserve moisture.*

established, and the compost normally holds moisture well to aid watering. However, grow-bags are not all of equal quality and growth results vary, so do take care to buy only recognised and recommended brands. Grow-bags are convenient, but they are not very attractive for a container garden hoping to double as a sophisticated outdoor lounging and dining area. You can disguise them by concealing them behind a low timber, stone or brick wall or batten, which effectively converts them into a kind of raised bed that looks good against a sunny wall or trellis. On a timber-decked patio, roof garden or upper balcony, drained water may also be a problem and this will have to be contained by standing the bags in specially designed troughs or trays.

Once fruits and vegetables develop, they can be heavy and plants may be damaged by the sheer weight of them; this is often a particular problem with high yield, compact varieties where leaves and stems can be quite overwhelmed. Special metal plant supports are available, designed to push down into the pot or grow-bag to offer support and keep the plant in a tidy shape. It makes sense to purchase

baskets; or small-leaved herbs in tiered containers. Otherwise, any suitable sized wooden tub or terracotta pot would do. They also look highly attractive as compact leafy plants studded with brightly-coloured fruits or vegetables are every bit as decorative as any ornamental, flowering species. Some edible varieties are particularly handsome, like the feathery foliage of carrots for example, or the strawberry's delicate-shaped leaves, tiny white flowers and luscious red fruits. Clever container kitchen gardeners mix flowers and herbs with their fruit and vegetables to dress them up a little and encourage fertilisation. If you select the simpler, old-fashioned cottage varieties, the combination can work very well indeed. Pot marigolds always add a cheery note and are supposed to discourage some pests from plants such as beans and tomatoes. Alternatively, grow deliberate culinary combinations to make harvesting easy; bush basil near the tomatoes, for example; marjoram with the green beans; or mint (in a separate container as it is invasive) near the peas. Grow-bags are popular for growing vegetables and fruits on patios and paved areas, incorporating a balanced selection of nutrients so plants will not need feeding until fairly

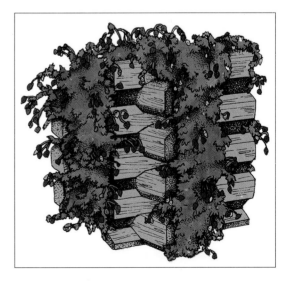

*Fig 82   An unusual style of strawberry planter, created using interlocking lengths of timber.*

Fig 83   Gravel trays will neatly constrain the overspill of grow-bags on roof gardens, patios and balconies.

and insert these while the plant is still young to ensure adequate support right from the early stages.

## Growing Vegetables

If you always imagined that growing vegetables involved a large expanse of double-dug soil and a lot of hard work, think again. Providing that the container is deep enough and the plants reasonably compact, most vegetables can be grown in pots or troughs to provide an attractive display and the pleasure of sampling your own produce from minimum space and effort. Naturally it makes sense to grow only your own particular favourites; or tender sun-loving treats such as baby courgettes or miniature tomatoes, novelty egg-sized white aubergines, 'Easter Egg', or brightly coloured peppers and chillis, which are all attractive plants. Don't waste precious space and resources trying to maximise on maincrop (and rather dull) vegetables like cabbages and potatoes; choose the more unusual types that tend to be expensive or difficult to obtain in the shops. Most of the top seed ranges offer a good choice of the latest salad varieties appearing in the best restaurants and top quality greengrocers, like radicchio and oak leaf lettuce, corn salad, chicory and endive – all of which are as easy to grow as garden

lettuce – and are almost ornamental with their frilled and coloured leaves.

Tubs, troughs, pots and grow-bags of rich compost in a sheltered, sunny position will grow delicious aubergines, tomatoes and courgettes. Dwarf varieties available include an aubergine only 7cm (3in) long and compact *Capsicum* plants producing red, green, yellow, black and white sweet peppers for colourful cooking. The tiny cherry tomato types are particularly versatile; grow them in strawberry pots or hanging baskets; for tubs and pots, choose a self-supporting variety. A good tip with tomatoes is to leave a gap between the top of the soil and the rim of the container to facilitate generous watering.

Dwarf varieties of peas and beans can be grown quite easily in pots and planters and do not require elaborate staking and the purple types are particularly attractive. Alternatively, grow runner beans as an ornamental climber in a patio or balcony garden. The bright green leaves and vivid red or orange flowers are remarkably attractive – the edible beans a mere bonus. Train them on wires or strings between your container and a wall or fence, or insert a wigwam-style support in the pot for a free-standing display. Familiar salad vegetables grow quickly and are easily incorporated with other plants as an extra, mini crop; or planted in succession in small boxes or pots to supply the kitchen from late spring to early autumn. Miniature cucumbers 20cm (8in) long can be trained up trellis above the pot and different shaped radishes can be planted in the smallest containers. Plant spring onion sets into troughs or window-boxes in mid-spring with the tip of the bulb just showing above the compost, to be harvested in early autumn. Curly-leaved and other ornamental lettuces can be grown in single pots.

Even carrots and potatoes can be grown in the minimum of space on a patio or roof garden. Choose the round, stump-rooted carrot varieties like 'Parmex' which are ideal for shallow soils, producing an almost circular vegetable with a good flavour; seed potatoes should be reduced to three shoots per tuber and planted in a large pot. Earthing up in late spring to early summer should produce a crop of new potatoes in mid-summer.

## Growing Fruit

Much as we love the convenience and flavour of home-grown fruit, we are frequently reluctant to spare the space for shady trees or straggling bushes. The secret is to turn them into an ornamental feature by confining them in pots, clipping, pruning and training them into formal shapes, and treating the fruits as a decorative and delicious bonus. Soft fruit can often be grown in single pots and pruned as a modest bush or trained on wires. Raspberry canes take up very little room and do well in a sunny spot; blackberries and loganberries can be trained in fans on wires arranged at 1, 1.5 and 2m (3, 5 and 6ft) heights above the pot or along an adjoining wall or fence. Red- and whitecurrant are also good fruits to be trained as fans; blackcurrants grow on the young wood so are better pruned into compact bushes producing as much as 4.5kg (10lb) of fruit per bush. You can also grow gooseberries in tubs, as bushes or as single stem cordons.

Fruit trees, with their pretty foliage and fine flowers are excellent small decorative specimens for growing in pots. Dwarf varieties can be trained into formal shapes or, where space is really limited, into the two-dimensional effect of cordons and espaliers where the branches are trained along horizontal wires. Often peaches, apricots and nectarines are available ready trained in fan shapes, but these require shelter and plenty of sunshine to fruit. Pruning in winter to maintain the shape, and again in summer to control new growth, is all that is really required once the trees are established. Apples and pears grow well in containers, but you will need to buy a couple of compatible varieties for fertilisation, unless several types have been grafted on to the one trunk. A fig particularly enjoys being grown in a pot where the restriction of its roots encourages the tree to fruit. It likes a warm, sunny position, preferably fan-trained against a sheltered wall.

Fruit trees should be protected from frosts in winter by covering them in sacking; growing them in pots means you can also experiment with more tender species, to be brought inside to a light, well-ventilated conservatory or

*Fig 84   A pear tree* (Pyrus communis).

Fig 85   *Herbs are ideal for pot growing.*

covered terrace in winter. Standard-trained citrus trees – a ball of pretty bright green foliage, with scented white flowers and glowing fruits on top of a slender trunk – grown in Versailles tubs, are a classic for formal gardens.

Strawberries are the perfect and most popular patio fruit. Plants are attractive with their fresh green leaves and red fruits, and providing they are given good drainage and a humus-rich soil, will flourish in pots and containers, hanging baskets and special strawberry planters or barrels, designed to carry a large number of plants on the minimum of ground space. You can make your own strawberry container out of an old barrel by drilling drainage holes in the bottom and making a series of small holes in several rows around the sides. These should be no lower than 60cm (24in) from the base of the

barrel and the rows of holes should be staggered. Fill with John Innes No 3 potting mixture, with a 5cm (2in) perforated zinc tube in the centre of the first row of holes for easy watering. Insert the strawberry plants in the holes and grow in a sunny position, feeding with fertiliser once growth starts.

## Herbs

Herbs make wonderful pot-grown plants for window-boxes, large planters and small individual containers. Their soft, natural colours, aromatic foliage and delicate flowers offer such variety of shape, form and shade, that you could easily create an exciting container garden exclusively from herb species, conjuring up a relaxing cottage-style patio or Mediterranean roof garden, or you could design a special culinary or medicinal herbal collection. Alternatively, they combine well with other plants such as vegetables or informal country-style containers planted with roses and carnations, night-scented stocks and Sweet Williams or standard trained marguerites. The majority of herbs prefer plenty of sunshine and good drainage, although there are some shade-tolerant leafy species for darker corners. Annuals should be replaced every year by growing from seed or buying young plants, while tender perennials such as rosemary and bay may have to be overwintered indoors in severe weather.

The more compact, lower growing or self-supporting bushy species of herbs are best for growing in pots, from the tiny-leaved thymes offering a great many variegated and coloured forms with differing scents, to spiky chives with their purple powder puff flowers and the soft, felty grey or purple leaves of the sages. With their subtle colouring and wide variety of leaf shapes and sizes, pink, blue, purple and lilac flowers, all seem perfectly compatible and you can happily combine your own favourites for the kitchen or devise a decorative scheme for a scented and relaxing seating area guaranteed to be busy with bees and butterflies.

# CHAPTER 4

# Practical Planting

You now have your plants, either grown from seed or recently purchased, selected according to your planting plan for compatability of soil, light, heat and watering needs, to provide your container garden with colour harmonies and contrasts of size and shape. The site is right for sun and shade and everything is at hand – take care not to ruin all your careful planning with careless planting.

## CHOOSING AND USING COMPOST

One of the big advantages of growing plants in containers is that you are completely in control of the growing medium so that you can ensure it is free from disease and pests, that it has exactly the correct pH balance for the plant's preference and that the soil is rich and moisture retaining, or poorer and free-draining according to requirements. This all helps your plant to flourish and provides the opportunity to enjoy some of the more fussy species that you may not otherwise be able to grow in the garden because your conditions are not right. Real lime-haters like azaleas, rhododendrons and some heathers, will not tolerate chalk or any form of alkali in the soil and despite digging-in or top dressing with supplements, will not flourish in the long term.

The disadvantage of container gardening is that this perfectly formulated soil resource is exhaustible and, once established, plants will require regular feeding, especially during the growing season. Small containers growing a large number of plants in a dense arrangement,

like hanging baskets, will need complete compost replacement every year. Limited depth of soil also means that moisture evaporates rapidly so all but the largest containers will need conscientious watering, maybe twice a day during particularly hot weather, or where containers are in a hot, dry, sunny situation. Providing that you do not neglect watering and feeding your containers, restricting the roots of plants will do them no harm; in the case of pot-grown shrubs and trees, this can be a useful technique for limiting the size of the specimen to manageable proportions suitable for displaying on a patio or other small, paved area. Large, permanent plants can also be gently turned out and have their roots clipped or pruned in order to limit their size and to prevent them from becoming root-bound.

Container growing is useful for invasive plants that you may be reluctant to introduce to the garden proper with their tendency to become unmanageable and swamp other specimens. A large pot or planter would be a good way to keep a collection of mints under control, for example; to grow an elegant clump of bamboo; or, in well-moistened soil, one of the rather vigorous marginal plants normally grown at the side of a pond or pool. Proprietary potting composts are specially formulated to suit a plant's particular needs and ordinary garden soil should never be used to plant up your containers. Garden soil is unsterilised, quite probably full of pests and weed seeds, and is unlikely to be of the correct consistency needed for good drainage.

There are two main types of compost. First, soil-based, which is largely sterilised loam with

Fig 86    The Gerbera *will grow well in John Innes potting compost No.2 and then in ordinary well-drained soil.*

the addition of peat, sand and nutrients, marketed as John Innes mixtures and numbered for different applications: No 1 for giving young plants a good start; No 2 for good general purpose use; No 3 or 4 for large plants or those which prefer a rich soil. Plants in soil-based composts require feeding less regularly; drainage is good and the compost holds moisture better so it is less likely to dry out or require excessive watering in dry weather. Some loam composts perform better than others and it is important to purchase a recommended brand.

The second type, soil-less composts, are peat-based and tend to be much lighter, making them particularly suited to areas where weight may be a problem such as balconies or roof gardens. Lightness may not be an advantage with large plants which may not be stable,

especially in an exposed site or where the tub itself is made of a light material. Those composts based entirely on peat are the lightest, while others have sand or grit added to give more weight to the containers and to improve drainage. Soil-less composts do not hold the water well and will need watering regularly. Should they completely dry out, they are very difficult to moisten again so this should be avoided at all costs. Drainage is also not as good as with soil-based composts and equal care should be taken not to overwater, or the compost may become irretrievably waterlogged. Soil-less composts tend to be less expensive but will require feeding more often. Some plants, as already mentioned, have special requirements; *ericaceous* or lime-hating species such as camellias and rhododendrons must be given an acid or lime-free mixture, while cacti and orchids also have very special needs and the composts used must be strictly formulated to suit their requirements. One way to help your budget, particularly when planting up large containers, is to mix up your own compost. This is quite easily done by buying the separate ingredients, weighing or measuring them out into a trough or mixing tray and turning them over several times with your trowel until they are thoroughly mixed. You can buy packs of the appropriate nutrient chemicals, ready mixed, from most garden centres, to incorporate in your own loam or peat-based mixture. Do not forget to omit the chalk if you are intending to plant lime-hating species.

## John Innes Compost Mixtures

### Seed Compost

Mix together two parts light or medium sterilised loam, one part granulated moss and one part sharp, horticultural sand – the lime-free type, and to each bushel, that is 8 gallons (36 litres), add 42g (1.5oz) of superphosphate and 21g (0.75oz) of chalk or ground limestone.

## Potting Compost

**John Innes No 1**   Mix seven parts of the loam with three parts of the peat and two parts of the sand, and to each bushel add 113g (4oz) of John Innes base fertiliser available in packs from your local garden centre and 21g (0.75oz) of chalk or ground limestone. Base fertiliser, should you wish to mix that yourself also, comprises, by weight, two part hoof and horn, 1/8in grist, which contains 13 per cent nitrogen, two parts calcium phosphate and one part potassium sulphate.

**John Innes Mixtures Nos 2–3**   Double the quantities of fertiliser mix and of chalk to make John Innes No 2; and treble them for No 3.

## Soil-Less or Peat-Based Composts

### Seed Compost

Mix together one part moist peat, one part dry sand, or grit – for a special light compost, use synthetic perlite or vermiculite instead – and to each bushel add a recommended proprietary fertiliser mix recommended for soil-less composts.

### Potting Compost

To three parts peat and one part sand, grit, perlite or vermiculite, add the appropriate compost fertiliser base for potting compost as instructed; or make up your own mix by combining thoroughly to each bushel 85g (3oz) of ammonium nitrate, 28g (1oz) of potassium sulphate, 85g (3oz) of hoof and horn, 57g (2oz) of magnesium limestone (Dolomite), 113g (4oz) of chalk and 57g (2oz) of calcium superphosphate. To convert this mixture for lime-hating plants, omit the chalk and add a little acid loam and some leaf mould to create an excellent mixture requiring no extra fertiliser. This is particularly good for growing camellias.

## Compost for Cacti

Cacti – and your alpines, need an extremely well drained and aerated compost. This can be easily made by adding an extra third of sharp sand to your John Innes No 2 potting compost mixture.

*Fig 87   Small collection of cacti and succulents including* Sempervivum.

## Compost for Bulbs

Bulbs will grow perfectly well outdoors in containers of general purpose compost. However, specially formulated bulb fibres are available for special pots or window-boxes and comprise mainly a mixture of peat, oyster shell and charcoal.

## SUCCESSFUL PLANTING

Good provision for drainage and care not to damage the plants are the secrets of success when planting up containers. The container should incorporate drainage holes in the bottom and it may be necessary to drill extra holes where you feel that there are not enough, or where you are employing a container of your own devising, such as a barrel or box. To prevent the drainage holes from becoming clogged with soil, you should incorporate a layer of stones or crocks (pieces of broken pot) of about 2.5cm (1in). Where drainage holes are not possible, increase the drainage layer to about a third of the container's size. On top of this, add a 2.5cm (1in) layer of rough peat or leaf mould to prevent compost washing down through your crocks. Containers can be placed directly on a hard firm surface such as patio paving, but raising them slightly on blocks or bricks will improve drainage and protect the surface. Containers standing on grass, soil, timber decking or an area without an integral drainage system such as a balcony or roof garden, should be supplied with drip trays or saucers.

When ready for planting, add enough of the appropriate compost to the container, so that when the plant is inserted you will have room to add around 1.2cm (0.5in) of new compost on top of the plant's existing rootball and a gap of around 2.5cm (1in) from the top of the container for watering. Firm down the potting compost without compacting it; soil-less composts require less firming than loam-based. The aim is to plant your specimen with as little disturbance as possible, so if you are planting several plants in a single container, make sure you are ready to do them all at the same time. Try not to leave plants waiting to be planted in draughty corners or the hot back seat of a car for too long. If the existing soil around the plant seems very dry, immerse the whole rootball in a bucket of water for about an hour or until no more bubbles appear on the surface, before draining and planting. Plants are often damaged simply by removing them from their nursery container, so to minimise damage to roots, stems or leaves, support the stem of the plant gently between your fingers, tip up, and in the case of a rooted pot, tap the rim firmly on a solid surface and slide the plant out gently. If this does not work, try soaking the compost as described, still in its pot and, as a last resort, carefully clip or cut away the pot. Plants in black plastic should be slit down one side of the bag with a sharp knife, continuing the cut underneath so that the plastic can be easily peeled away from the rootball.

Position the plant where required in the container and adjust the level of compost if necessary. Gently add compost between the rootball and the side of the container, firming it down as you go (only lightly for soil-less compost). Top with around 1.2cm (0.5in) of new compost making sure that you do not get soil on the leaves or green stem and water thoroughly, checking that the drainage is good and the soil does not remain waterlogged.

Shrubs and trees may be supplied with the roots wrapped in sacking or polythene and bedding plants such as wallflowers may also be supplied tied in bundles and bare rooted, or sold *en masse* in trays or strips to be carefully lifted and divided. Take care that roots do not get damaged in transit, storage or planting. Plant bare rooted specimens by gently spreading the roots and holding the plant in position with the roots dangling down. It is a good idea to take a close look at root growth before planting, removing any dead material with a pair of sharp secateurs and reducing roots that are too long by up to one-third if necessary. Trickle the compost between the roots, firming it as you go and making sure that there are no air pockets. The plant should rest at exactly the same level of compost as before – indicated by a soil mark on the stem. Again, water until it runs out of the bottom of the container to encourage the compost to settle round the roots, but do not leave it standing in water.

*Fig 88    Well-planted, thriving window-boxes need thoughtful provision for drainage.*

Bulbs should be planted to the recommended depth, closely spaced but not touching to produce a mass of blooms. Top with compost between and above and gently firm in position, making sure to leave a watering space at the top.

## PLANTING UP WINDOW-BOXES

Drainage holes are not essential for window-boxes, and may indeed not be desirable because of the mess and damage they might cause. The best option is an inner container or liner with drainage holes incorporated so that any excess water filters through on to a layer of gravel or small stones in the main box. Put a good layer of drainage material such as stones or crocks in the bottom of the box or liner – around 5cm (2in) should be sufficient. Cover with a layer of coarse peat or moss as described above, then add a good water-retaining compost. Some people prefer to use a soil-less mixture because it is clean to handle and lightweight, putting less of a strain on your wall brackets. Plant your specimens as described, taking particular care to leave a gap at the top to avoid spills when watering and remember that soil should be renewed annually. Alternatively, plants need not be directly inserted, but left in rigid pots and packed with damp peat within the window-box. Thus plants can be easily removed and replaced as required, but take care to provide good provision for drainage in the bottom of the boxes.

*Fig 89    Summer Showers is a pretty geranium ideally suited to hanging baskets, where its delicate flowers and foliage make a dense display.*

## PLANTING UP HANGING BASKETS

Hanging baskets are usually made of wire or wooden slats so plants can be inserted between and allowed to cascade out of the sides. The basket should be lined with sphagnum moss or a pre-formed synthetic liner, with a small saucer of stones between your lining material and the soil to help retain moisture. Alternatively, plastic sheeting can be used as a liner, punctured with holes for drainage, but this does not look very attractive and is often used in conjunction with a thin layer of moss between the plastic sheet and basket. Fill with a peat-based potting compost that will hold the moisture well, since hanging baskets are prone to drying out rapidly. Leave a watering space of about 2.5cm (1in) at the top. Trailing plants can be inserted into the

sides of the container for an attractive mass of flowers and foliage, and also into the top of the container, keeping taller specimens to the centre of the arrangement. You may find it easier to get someone (preferably someone strong as it will get very heavy!) to hold the basket for you while you fill it; or suspend it from a low hook; or support the basket on a large flower pot. Take care not to behead your young plants when you lift up the supporting chain to hang the basket in its place. There are solid hanging containers available in terracotta or plastic, many of which incorporate a built-in drip tray or water reservoir. Plants will naturally have to be inserted from the top, with the taller upright plants to the centre and the trailing plants around the sides. A completed basket should be well watered before hanging. Wall baskets and pots should be planted in the same way.

CHAPTER 5

# Plant Maintenance

As the soil supply is limited, plants grown in containers do need a little extra maintenance. The compost is prone to drying out and nutrients may become exhausted, so watering and feeding must be a regular task. This commitment can be considerably reduced by careful management and the use of special techniques such as mulching to reduce moisture loss and automatic watering or feeding systems.

## WATERING

Incorrect watering – allowing the compost to dry out completely or waterlogging the soil so that roots or stems rot – is a common cause of failure in container-grown plants. Unfortunately a rigid watering regime does not provide the solution, since requirements depend directly on the size of pot, type of compost, the needs of the plant, a sunny or shady location, and daily weather conditions. Containers in an exposed sunny site will obviously need watering more frequently and the most vulnerable hanging baskets and window-boxes may need watering twice a day in warm weather. Small pots dry out more rapidly than large ones and plants in terracotta or clay containers will also need watering more frequently.

Plants which are allowed to dry out too thoroughly may never recover, and should never be left until they are seen to wilt. In particular, peat-based potting mixtures should never be allowed to dry out completely as they are very difficult to re-moisten. Sticking your finger into the soil about 1·3cm (0·5in) deep gives a quick indication of whether the compost

has dried out too far and needs watering. The top of the compost will also look much lighter if it has begun to dry out right through. A more accurate indication will be given by a moisture meter which normally features a probe to be pushed into the soil, with a simple dial above indicating whether it is dry, moist or wet.

A moisture meter may be useful to eliminate indecision and the temptation to water 'just in case'. Over-watering can be as disastrous for the majority of plants as too little moisture and you should always wait until the compost has started to dry out again. You should be able to distinguish between compost which is evenly moist and that which is wet and waterlogged. Only semi-aquatic species like rushes and reeds can tolerate these conditions.

*How* you water your containers is as important as spotting *when* to do it. It is no good simply moistening the top of the compost; the container needs a good soak so that the water reaches the roots. The best time to water is in the early morning or in the evening, taking care not to splash water on the foliage, or they may scorch in the hot sun of the day. Never allow water to stand in the saucer or drip tray below the plant. An arrangement of several containers is best served by a hosepipe with an adjustable spray nozzle which will quickly provide as much water as you need and can be easily controlled. A watering can with a long spout is useful for containers or hanging baskets which are difficult to reach, but entails a lot more extra work for watering large containers so may encourage under-watering. Watering hanging baskets or pots is always a problem, seemingly depositing as much water on your head as in the compost.

The answer is to invest in a watering lance or a special spray device designed for the purpose.

Where plants have similar watering needs and you are unable to give them regular attention, you can use an automatic watering system in spring and summer when reasonably fine weather can be guaranteed. This usually involves drip feeding plants with water from a reservoir bag or from the mains water supply using a header tank fitted with a ball-cock valve. There are also automatic controls which can be fitted to the water tap to turn it on every day for a set period of time or, better still, a pre-set volume of water.

You should also give some thought to the water you are using. Tap water is obviously most convenient, but if it contains a lot of lime (that is, you are in a 'hard' water area), it can damage alkaline-hating plants like many heathers and primulas, rhododendrons, azaleas or camellias. Wherever possible water such plants with rainwater collected in a clean butt, or buy and fit a water softening system to your outside supply: there are various devices on the market.

Mulching can help to reduce moisture loss and is a valuable technique for use with containers. Any exposed areas of soil should be covered with small pebbles, bark chips, moss or peat, especially while plants are young and prone to leaving bare areas. This will also eliminate weeds and looks highly attractive into the bargain.

# FEEDING

When plants have established themselves and are well rooted they will begin to exhaust the nutrients in container compost. Soil-based composts will need feeding less frequently and not as soon as soil-less or peat-based types. Plants require nitrogen for good growth, phosphorous for root development and potassium for the production of flowers and fruit and to encourage resistance to disease. These elements are only useful in their fixed form as nitrates, phosphates and potash. Other trace elements are required, including magnesium and iron. These plus the three main food requirements are available in different proportions to make up proprietary fertilisers for different plant needs. For example, a non-flowering plant needs plenty of nitrogen; flowering plants require plenty of potash; while phosphates are important to seedlings and young plants.

Fertilisers are generally divided into synthetics or organics. Synthetic chemicals act more quickly and are absorbed directly through the plant's roots. Organic fertilisers, produced by the rotted remains of dead plants and animal waste, are longer lasting. Among the organics, manure combines a balance of nutrients, but is not really practical for applying to hanging baskets or window-boxes. Nitrogen-rich dried blood, or hoof and horn, are easier to handle as are bone and fish meal, which are good sources of phosphates. Generally, fertilisers are applied to containers in 'single' or 'compound' form. Single fertilisers contain a particular plant food to give a special boost. For example, sulphate of ammonia contains 21 per cent nitrogen for producing better leaf growth; superphosphate provides 18 per cent phosphorous; and sulphate of potash supplies 48 per cent potash.

More commonly used are the compound fertilisers which are a special balanced mixture of all these elements, sometimes containing a blend of both organic and synthetic ingredients. The proportions are represented by the initials 'N' for nitrogen, 'P' for phosphorous and 'K' for potash — always in that order. For example, a 5:9:6 mixture has been found particularly suitable for roses, while 7:7:7 is a good even balance for vegetables, and a tomato fertiliser might be broken down into 4 per cent nitrogen, 4 per cent phosphorous and 7 per cent potash. Read the packet or container for its best use and how it should be applied.

*Fig 90   Be careful not to damage lime-hating plants like azaleas with ordinary tap water.*

Fig 91   Feeding methods. (a) Liquid fertiliser is simply diluted in the watering can to make a quick and convenient method of application. (b) Solid fertilisers are mixed into the top layer of the potting mixture to release their nutrients more slowly, and are longer acting. (c) Foliar feeds are sprayed on to the plant leaves for a quick pick-me-up effect. (d) Special fertiliser pills and sticks are buried in the compost for a slow release of nutrients over longer periods.

Fertilisers can be applied by a variety of methods. Liquid types are faster acting and solid fertilisers are slower and longer acting so do not need to be applied so frequently. Plants will only require feeding during the growing season, from spring through to autumn as appropriate. Over-feeding causes a build up of salts around the roots and damages the plant. Only established plants require feeding, around eight weeks after planting in their container. It is important to follow the manufacturer's instructions to the letter and not to apply a concentrated dose in the belief that it will do more good. A little diluted fertiliser at regular inter-vals is always better than a sudden blitz of high concentration and is less likely to cause damage. Always wear protective gloves when handling fertiliser and take care not to splash it on leaves and flowers, unless using one of the powdered or spray kinds recommended for that purpose. Established plants are normally fed once a fortnight during the growing season, but permanent, mature specimens may need feeding every week. Never feed a sick or over-dry plant hoping it will perk up; wait until it has recovered. Flowering climbers will need feeding carefully if they are not to produce too much foliage and few flowers.

Liquid fertiliser is normally diluted to the recommended dose and added to the compost when watering. It is also available as a foliar feed which can be sprayed directly on to the leaves – something not generally recommended as ordinary liquid fertilisers can damage foliage. However, these special formulations are quickly absorbed and are useful for giving a boost to an ailing plant. They are not to be considered a substitute for a general fertiliser applied to the compost.

Solid fertilisers are generally supplied in granular or powdered form which is sprinkled over the surface of the compost. Also available are fertiliser spikes and tablets which are pushed down into the compost to release their contents slowly over a period of several weeks, so that feeding has to be carried out less often. Mature, large plants benefit from being top dressed at the beginning of the growing season. The top 2·5cm (1in) layer of compost is removed and replaced with fresh mixture to which a little fertiliser has been added. This is a useful technique for a plant that can no longer be potted on or which has reached its required size.

# REPOTTING AND POTTING-ON

Plants do not like to be grown in containers that are too large and a small, young specimen in a huge pot will also look out of proportion. Eventually, many plants will outgrow their containers and require moving to larger pots or reducing in size, although this of course does not apply to the majority of seasonal plants such as spring bulbs and summer annuals which are simply removed and replaced when past their best.

When a larger, permanent plant has filled its container with roots, it is generally moved on to a larger pot of fresh compost to provide more room and more nutrients for growth. This is called potting-on. It is advisable to pot-on a plant before it outgrows its container and the compost becomes completely packed with roots. Under these conditions the plant is pot-bound and will begin to show signs of distress through lack of growth or general poor condition. The ideal time to pot-on is in early spring before the plant begins its vigorous season of growth; but fast-growing plants may also require potting-on during the summer, particularly if well fed.

To check how dense the root growth has become within the container, you may have to inspect the rootball, but if roots are already growing out of the drainage holes of your container, this will not be necessary for you will know at once that the plant is root-bound. To

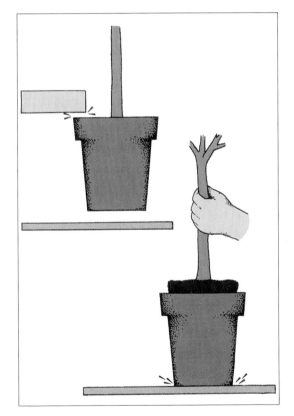

*Fig 92   To remove a tree from its pot and check root growth, ensure the rootball is moist and rap sharply on the rim with a wooden pole or batten, then lift carefully from the pot.*

87

turn a plant out of its pot, turn it up holding the stem lightly between your fingers. If you tap the rim of the pot sharply on the edge of a firm surface, plant and rootball should slide out easily for inspection. Sometimes root growth will be so advanced that little soil will remain around the coiled and matted mass. It may take two people to check a large plant with one person to tap the rim of the container with a wooden batten or similar object and the other gently to pull out the plant and rootball.

Potting-on requires a new pot with about 3.8cm (1.5in) of extra space for root growth. Plants may be moved to the next size or two of container, but no more than this or the pot will be too large. A large amount of compost around a plant's roots tends to discourage growth and may remain too moist after watering. Containers must be cleaned well before use and clay or terracotta pots soaked overnight in clean water. Add a layer of drainage material and suitable potting mixture as described on page 80. Position your plant in its required position allowing 2.5cm (1in) at the top for watering. The compost should cover the roots but keep it away from any area of green stem or foliage.

Large perennial plants cannot be potted-on endlessly and will eventually reach the size of plant and container that you require. When these plants begin to be root-bound – and this may occur annually depending on how vigorously they grow – they must be repotted to maintain health and good growth. Repotting involves removing the plant from its pot and reducing the size of the rootball by gently pulling away as much as 5cm (2in) of the old compost, cutting away any dead roots and generally pruning back. The plant should then be repotted in fresh compost in a pot the same size as the one from which it has been removed. Wash the container thoroughly and allow it to dry before re-using. The best time to repot is during a plant's rest period, before the growing season starts.

After repotting or potting-on, plants should be well watered in order to moisten but not saturate the compost. Where a plant is too large to remove from its container, top dressing should help maintain good growth. This involves removing the top 5cm (2in) of soil in spring and replacing it with fresh compost.

## TRAINING AND PRUNING

Plants grown in containers need to be well shaped and in good condition to maintain an attractive display. Deadheading annuals not only removes unsightly material, but also encourages a continuous display of blooms and reduces the likelihood of disease. Deadheading ornamental plants such as roses and camellias will also encourage further blooms. If you have herbaceous plants in your containers, remove dead top growth promptly at the end of the growing season. Keep taller plants and climbers looking tidy during the growing season with supports such as canes, stakes and wire frames which can be tied in as the plant grows. It is important not to tie too tightly around stems or you may not allow them the space to grow and they will be damaged if cut into. There are various forms of trellis and frameworks available including pyramids and fan shapes which are suitable for climbing plants grown in containers to make a special vertical display.

To improve the shape of some half hardy annuals and perennials like fuchsias and dahlias, pinch out the growing tip to encourage bushy growth. Removing surplus shoots or stems can also produce a better quality plant and more flowers with climbers like jasmine, whose old stems should be thinned out in the winter or early spring.

Shrubs and small trees grown in containers may require pruning to a neater or more decorative shape to suit your design plans. As a general rule though, pruning should be kept to a minimum, particularly when plants are young. If a shrub produces flowers on a previous season's growth, it should not be pruned until

*Fig 93   Fuchsias are easily shaped by pinching out the growing tips.*

flowering has finished, by removing any untidy growth and cutting back to the required shape. The plant can be thinned by removing shoots just above soil level. Where a plant flowers on stems formed in the same season, you should prune early in the year before it starts its new growth, when it can be cut back to almost ground level.

Climbers can be approached in a similar way, although vigorous plants like jasmine may need extensive pruning to avoid a tangled mass of stems. Evergreen climbers should be pruned in early spring and deciduous types in winter. Wisteria is normally pruned in mid-summer when the side shoots are cut back to about 15cm (6in), and in mid-winter when they are

*Fig 94   Fig trees, as well as producing fruit, have attractive foliage.*

shortened to two buds. Clematis should be pruned according to their kind and you should check with your supplier on particular requirements. Roses require quite careful pruning based on general principles. You should always prune to an outward pointing bud to keep the centre of the plant open. The best time to prune is in early spring when hybrid tea roses can be cut right back to two or six buds from the base, while the more vigorous floribundas should be pruned less severely for plenty of blooms. Prune climbing roses by cutting back the side shoots to within one or three buds of the main stem. Ramblers should be cut back completely as soon as flowering has finished.

Plants clipped into formal shapes look particularly attractive grown in containers and slow-growing, small-leaved evergreens such as box, privet and yew are excellent subjects for this. Larger-leaved types such as bay and holly can also be artificially shaped. The technique requires patience and some skill, but beginners can easily achieve simple shapes such as pyramids, cones and orbs. Shapes will need to be clipped at the end of the summer. Topiary forms are available ready-grown, but these are expensive.

A large number of shrubby or semi-shrubby plants can be trained to form standards where a mass of foliage is carried on top of a long tall stem. This looks particularly attractive in a pot or container as part of a formal patio or terrace arrangement. Geraniums, roses, begonias, fuchsias and fruit trees are all popular subjects for this treatment. To create a standard you generally grow on from a rooted cutting, removing all the side shoots, but not the foliage, on the main stem. When the plant reaches the required height, take off the top and allow side shoots to develop, pinching out the growing tips of the shoots to encourage bushiness. When the head of the plant reaches the shape and size you want, remove the foliage on the supporting stem.

Fruit trees and bushes require quite specific pruning in order to produce fruit satisfactorily. Fruit varieties grown in containers may also have to be trained into artificial and decorative forms to limit size and shape. Regular pruning involves the removal of fruiting stems to make way for new cropping growth in the case of soft fruits like raspberries and blackcurrants and some tree fruits like peaches, grapes and apricots. Some soft fruits like gooseberries and redcurrants produce fruits on side shoots from the main branches, so the main framework should be maintained with only surplus growth cut out in summer and winter. Apples and pears are pruned in a similar manner by shortening the side shoots twice a year. Check in a specialist book for details if you are keen to maintain maximum fruit yields and a neat healthy plant.

Young fruit trees are often trained into a particular shape or framework which makes them easier to manage and more decorative. To allow *soft* fruit to grow as a bush, you should prune with an aim to producing an even arrangement of branches radiating from a main stem. This can be done by cutting back the young branches on a rooted cutting in its first spring to about 12–15cm (5–6in) from the base. The following spring, shorten each shoot that grows from the buds in the same way, to double up again. *Top* fruit varieties are made into bushes in the same way by cutting back to 45cm (18in) to stimulate side shoots, each being cut back to 30–45cm (12–18in) from its base to double the number of branches. Repeat until you have the framework you require.

Two-dimensional frameworks are great space savers for container-grown fruit in small areas. The cordon has single or multiple stems which can be trained vertically, horizontally or at an angle. To create a single stem *soft* fruit

cordon, the top bud is allowed to grow and all lower buds and shoots removed. This main stem is cut back by half every winter until the required height is reached, then the side shoots are pruned twice a year as normal. To create a single stem *top* fruit cordon, the graft is cut back to about 30cm (1ft) and the extension to the leading shoot is shortened by half each year to stimulate side shoots. These side shoots and the leading shoot are pruned as normal twice a year once the cordon has reached the required height. To make a *multiple* cordon you allow two or more shoots to develop at the top. These are tied in place and shortened to upward-facing buds in winter from which vertical or slanting stems will grow and should be around 30–38cm (12–15in) apart.

An espalier is another useful training technique for small spaces, producing a regular arrangement of horizontal arms usually against wires on a wall or wooden trellis. The arms are trained as cordons by cutting the stem of the tree to the level of the first wire or support, just above three good buds. The buds will produce shoots which are trained with the centre shoot vertical and a shoot on either side at an angle of 45°. These arms are lowered to a horizontal position in the following winter and pruned to about two-thirds. The vertical shoot is cut to the next wire in the same manner for the following season. Side shoots on the main branches should be pruned as usual twice a year. A tier will be produced each year until you have the number of branches you require; then allow only two stems to grow and train them to each side along the top wire.

Trees and soft fruits will do very well and produce plenty of fruit against a sunny wall or trellis, yet take up very little space when trained as fans with the branches tied in an even fan shape to enjoy maximum sunshine. Cut back the plant to 30–45cm (12–18in) from the ground and tie the branches in to a fan shape, then prune to 20–30cm (8–12in) to encourage a framework of fruiting branches. Any branches growing towards or away from the

Fig 95    *These mature cyclads are balanced by the heavy stone pots in which they are growing.*

wall should be cut away. The young branches are trained to fan out symmetrically without forcing. If the lower branches are reluctant to go into position, they can be tied to canes fixed at an angle and lowered gradually during the growing season.

A weeping or festoon fruit tree such as an apple, pear or plum makes a decorative feature and maintains a small-sized tree without encouraging the fruiting side shoots which would develop if you merely cut off the tall stems. The tree is allowed to grow without pruning to the height you require, when the leading shoot and any long side shoots are encouraged to bend right over and are secured to the trunk of the tree. Further branches which are long enough can be treated in the same way in the following year. Any side shoots appearing along the trained branches of apples and pears should be pruned in summer to

produce fruiting spurs. The arched branches are pruned as for cordons; but for plum trees the side shoots are left to grow and fruit until long enough to tie down or cut out to make way for new shoots. In time, the main branches will become permanently curved and the ties can be removed.

## WINTER AND HOLIDAY CARE

Container-grown plants should need very little care through winter. Once dead herbaceous material and finished annuals have been tidied away, remaining plants will require little feeding or watering during the colder, dormant season. Tender plants such as citrus trees and non-hardy, sub-tropical species can be brought indoors or moved to a more sheltered position at the first sign of frost. Plants left outside in containers may be prone to root damage from being frozen so unless they are in a sheltered position it is worth surrounding them with dry straw or bracken to prevent the compost from freezing. Small pots can be buried up to their rim in the garden, or you can pack them with soil, straw or peat in a much larger container to prevent freezing, yet without the risk of losing your winter display.

If you intend to go away on holiday or business during the summer months, you should arrange with a friend or neighbour to water your containers correctly in your absence (show them the guidelines on page 83). Alternatively, set up an automatic watering system supplied from a reservoir or the mains water supply. Pots could also be placed on a section of capillary matting with one end placed in a container of water. Containers in a particularly sunny spot could be moved to a slightly shadier position where a mulch of stones or peat will also help to slow down water evaporation. Before you go, water plants thoroughly and remove any flowers or buds about to open and cut away any dead or damaged foliage and clear away dead material.

92

CHAPTER 6

# Pests and Diseases

## GOOD HYGIENE AND MANAGEMENT

In the relatively controlled environment of the container garden, good management should keep soil-based diseases to a minimum. However, you cannot completely avoid trouble and infestation from air-borne insects and pests is virtually impossible to prevent. All you can do is maintain the best possible levels of hygiene by thoroughly scrubbing and drying containers before use every time, using only sterilised, fresh compost and removing dead plant material as soon as it is seen. Plants that do become infested or diseased should be treated or removed from the container with speed. Early treatment can often arrest what might develop into a serious problem or spread to other plants, so keep an eye open when watering or feeding. It is even a good idea to get into the habit of casting a glance over the general condition of your plants when lazing on the patio or terrace.

Good hygiene and prompt treatment will not only keep plants looking good, but will also keep necessary application of chemicals to a minimum. This you should aim for at all costs, without letting a problem get out of control, not just from an ecological point of view, but also for your own safety and the threat of resistance build-up. Sometimes simply picking off any bugs or hosing down a plant with soapy water will be sufficient in the early stages. Otherwise, use a proprietary treatment specially recommended for your particular problem — and there is a whole medicine chest of products available at local garden centres to cope with every eventuality. For safety and efficiency, all chemicals should be stored out of the reach of pets and children and be correctly labelled and if the instructions get washed off or go missing, discard the product. Also look out for shelf expiry dates as some chemicals can quickly lose their strength. Equally important is to follow the manufacturers' instructions to the letter. Never be tempted to increase the dose or dilution believing that it will work more quickly. Always wear rubber gloves and wash hands, sprayers and dishes thoroughly after use. Remember to keep children and pets indoors when spraying.

Fig 96   Lilies are generally hardy and look good as 'specimen' plants on the patio.

Ideally, insecticide and pesticide sprays should be applied only on a still day, preferably in the evening when bees are less active. Avoid spraying or dusting any plants with open flowers and always allow the recommended period to elapse between spraying and eating vegetables and fruits, washing them carefully before use.

There are a great many pests and diseases which can attack plant roots, foliage, flowers and fruits and the following checklists will give a guide to what you should be looking out for. For more specific problems such as clematis wilt, strawberry mildew or pea and bean weevil you should check an appropriate specialist reference book.

# SPOTTING THE PROBLEM

Keep an eye open for the following symptoms as an early warning that there is something wrong with your plant.

## Poor or Slow Growth

Growth slows down naturally during the winter or a plant's resting stage. However, if your annuals are slow to get away or summer growth is poor, you are probably over-watering or under-feeding. Pale leaves or leggy growth indicate under-feeding and a sun-loving plant that is not receiving sufficient light. Also check that the plant is not pot-bound and requires potting-on (described on page 87) as this is often a cause of poor growth.

## Leaf, Flower and Bud Drop

Shock to the plant will often cause leaves, buds or flowers to drop off, so treat specimens gently when moving or transplanting and never reposition in a spot with completely different light and warmth. Saturated or dried-out compost can also be a cause of this problem. Check that you are not over-feeding or using a feed with the incorrect balance for your particular plant. Flower buds can sometimes be eaten by birds.

## No Flowers

Buds that disappear or fail to open have probably been attacked by birds, weevils or caterpillars. If they refuse to appear altogether and the plant is making plenty of foliage, you may be over-feeding. The wrong light and warmth conditions could also inhibit flowering.

## Root Problems

The most common problem with roots is rot and this is frequently caused by over-watering, usually in cold damp weather, which encourages fungus to thrive. Roots may also be eaten or damaged by pests such as caterpillars, maggots and grubs which frequently affect vegetables and some flowering plants. The use of sterilised potting mixtures will help keep infestation to a minimum.

## Disfigured Flowers and Fruit

Blooms, particularly those of chrysanthemums, dahlias and other ornamental plants can be eaten by earwigs and caterpillars. Virus can attack some types of herbaceous plants resulting in uneven, streaked flower colour. Distorted flowers may indicate the presence of capsid bugs. Specific flowers may also suffer the mottled effect of petal blight (chrysanthemums and dahlias), blotch (delphiniums) or thrips (gladioli). Pest damage and fungus infestations will often distort or destroy edible fruits if left unsprayed. Caterpillars and beetles are common culprits, but tree fruits might also suffer from scab or rot, or from cracking and discoloration indicating insufficient watering and feeding. Soft fruits are prone to rot and mildew. If tree fruits tend to drop before maturing, this is an indication that they have either been poorly pollinated or insufficiently fed or watered.

## Vegetable Disorders

Since you will be using fresh compost every season, you should have no problem with the pest and disease build up in the soil which necessitates crop rotation in the main garden. However, less than conscientious watering will cause split, green blotchy patches or blossom-end rot in tomatoes; pea moths might strike your garden peas; slugs can destroy young plants; carrot fly attacks carrots, parsnips and parsley. If root vegetables are cracking, this is probably because you are not watering frequently enough. Brassicas tend to be prone to root infestation by aphids, bugs, maggots and grubs or can be affected by club root which swells and distorts them.

## Wilting Plants

A wilting plant usually indicates that the compost is too dry and watering, and spraying the leaves, should revive it. If the soil is sufficently moist, check the roots which may not be taking up enough moisture through rot or pests. Over-feeding can cause build up around the roots and this can damage them. Where roots and compost are not to blame, one answer is to move the plant into a cooler, shadier position.

## Leaves Turning Yellow

Occasionally a lower leaf might turn yellow and drop off, but if your plant looks generally pale and sickly or a large number of leaves start to turn yellow and drop, you are probably over-watering, or the plant is in an over-exposed position and is suffering from a draught. Yellowing leaves that do not fall indicate an incorrect compost balance and lime-hating plants that have been grown in too alkaline a mixture, or are being given 'hard' water. If your plants have poor growth and yellow leaves this indicates a lack of nutrients, so you should check your feeding.

## Brown Patches on Leaves

Dead brown patches appearing on foliage usually indicate frost damage or sunlight that is too strong. If this is not likely, you may be over-feeding or not providing enough potash in the soil. Also check that you have not splashed the leaves with liquid fertiliser or pesticide, or exposed the plant to the fumes from toxic timber treatments. Brown discoloration is often a sign of such diseases as scab, rust, black spot or infestation of mites.

## Mottled and Spotted Leaves

Mottling is a common symptom of virus disease which may also stunt and distort the plant. A virus may cause yellow stripes or blotches and look out for grey mould, white mildew, the silver mottling produced by thrips and the white flecks of leafhoppers. Froghoppers hide their young within blobs of white froth which can be easily hosed off before treatment. Foliage may also become spotted by spraying with an over-concentrated dilution of pesticide or from water droplets scorching the leaf in strong sunshine.

## Holes in Leaves

Holes in leaves are usually caused by insects such as caterpillars and earwigs, or slugs and snails. Particular plants may also be prone to capsid bugs, weevils and beetles. Roses and some other plants may be prone to leaf-cutter bees and slug worms. Trees in the *Prunus* species – plums, peaches and cherries – may develop brown patches and holes on the leaves if given insufficient water and nutrients.

## Distorted Leaves

Crinkled and oddly-shaped leaves indicate a virus infection. Trees, shrubs and some other plants may also contract a form of wilt which should be cut out and destroyed. Aphids can cause the leaves of some fruit trees to curl up and mites and sawflies will curl the leaves of many other plants. Careless use of weedkiller can leave plant leaves curled up and damaged. Peach leaf curl can affect peaches, nectarines and almonds.

## Shoot Disorders

Shoots can quickly become smothered with an infestation of aphids, scale insects and woolly aphids which can easily be seen by the naked eye. More difficult to spot are leopard moth caterpillars which burrow into the stems of many trees and shrubs causing the leaves to wilt; or cut worms which live in the soil and attack the shoots of vegetables and annuals. Shoots may also be infested with all kinds of rot, virus and other diseases such as leaf gall, canker, and scab-producing growths, wilting, spots and streaks which should be treated as soon as they are noticed.

# PESTS

Prompt treatment can prevent pests spreading and keep an infestation under control. Manufacturers' instructions will recommend which product is best suited for controlling a particular type of insect and many products are now claimed not to damage bees, ladybirds and other useful insects. Also look out for warnings that some chemicals cannot be used with certain plants such as chrysanthemums and fuchsias.

## Aphids

Aphids may be green, brown, black or grey, are easily seen with the naked eye and quickly build up a dense colony of insects that suck the plant's sap and stunt its growth with yellow distorted leaves. Aphids also secrete a sticky substance called honeydew which encourages the growth of black mould.

## Ants

Ants disturb plant roots by tunnelling through the soil and also transfer aphids from one plant to another.

Fig 97   Capsid bug.

## Capsid Bugs

Capsid bugs produce tattered holes in the young leaves of dahlias, beans, currants, forsythia and other plants.

## Cut Worms

Fat cut worm grubs live in the soil and eat the young shoots of vegetables and annual plants.

## Earwigs

Earwigs eat holes in petals and leaves during the night and live in nearby cracks or holes by day.

## Flea Beetle

The flea beetle produces tiny holes in the leaves of cabbage, radish, turnip, wallflower and related plants.

## Froghoppers

These small hopping insects produce a frothy white substance usually called cuckoo spit.

Fig 99    Red spider mite web.

Fig 98    Froghopper

## Leaf-cutter Bees

These attack plants such as roses, lilac, privet and laburnum, removing bite-sized semi-circles out of the leaf edges.

## Leafhoppers

Leafhoppers attack roses, geraniums, primulas and other plants, leaving white flecks on the leaves.

## Mealy Bugs

These small, grey woolly-looking insects lay a mass of eggs around buds and leaf stems.

## Red Spider Mite

Tiny reddish mites that are hard to see cause yellow mottling on leaves which eventually go brown and shrivel. A fine white web on the underneath of leaves may also be seen. Red spider mites are usually a result of hot dry conditions.

## Scale Insects

These small brown insects cluster on stems and leaves to suck the sap and weaken the plant. Like aphids they produce a tell-tale sticky honeydew.

## Sciarid-fly Maggots

Sometimes called fungus gnats, these tiny black-headed worms infest the soil in containers and eat the roots. They are encouraged by damp humid conditions.

## Slugs and Snails

Slugs and snails can easily destroy a young plant in a couple of bites. They thrive in dead material so keep the area tidy to inhibit breeding.

97

## Thrips

These tiny black-winged insects create white patches on the foliage and will fall out on to a sheet of white paper if you shake the plant gently.

## Vine Weevil

Small notches in the foliage of camellias, clematis, primulas, rhododendrons and other plants indicate the presence of vine weevils. Grubs also eat the roots.

## Whitefly

Small triangular whitefly cluster on the underside of leaves, suck the sap and create honeydew which turns the foliage yellow.

## Wood-lice

Wood-lice can cause a problem by damaging the roots and soft stems of plants.

## Mildew

There are various kinds of mildew which attack certain plants and produce a grey-white mould on stems, leaves and buds. It is often caused by over-crowding and over-watering.

## Rusts

Rusts are fungi creating reddish-brown spots or patches on foliage and there are many kinds which affect different plants.

## Virus Disease

A virus disease could cause mottled, streaked or distorted leaves, malformed flowers and uneven growth. It can be passed by handling infected plants and these should be destroyed immediately in order to prevent the infection spreading.

# DISEASES

A healthy plant which is well cared for will be better able to resist diseases, so you should ensure that yours are maintained in top condition. It is not always possible to spot and treat a disease in its early stages. If a plant is affected beyond salvation, it should be removed as swiftly as possible and burnt to prevent the disease spreading to other plants.

## Black Spot

These are black or brown spots on the leaves of roses which turn yellow and drop off.

## Botrytis

Sometimes called grey mould, botrytis is a furry fungus which mostly attacks indoor and conservatory plants. The plant will produce clouds of dust-like spores if disturbed or shaken.

Fig 100   Botrytis.

## Chlorosis

Acid-loving plants like rhododendrons and camellias may develop yellow veining between the leaves indicating that the soil is too alkaline and needs adjusting.

# Appendix – Plant Lists

## BACKBONE PLANTING

Shrubs, trees and climbers can all be grown in containers, although their size may be restricted. They add height and all-season interest to your scheme, plus the bonus of a special display at certain times of the year from blossom, to autumn colour and so on. These major plants will form your backbone planting, ideally augmented by interesting foliage plants, such as evergreens like ivies or species with strong architectural shapes like palms, bamboos, hostas or ferns.

## ORNAMENTAL TREES AND SHRUBS

Choose small, compact or dwarf species, in varieties that will offer maximum year-round interest. For specialist planting instructions, see page 80. To keep trees and shrubs in peak condition, regular watering, feeding and mulching will be necessary. Growing them in containers is the perfect opportunity to grow more tender species, bringing them into more sheltered areas at the onset of colder weather. Heights shown are intended to offer a rough guide only.

**Plant** *Abelia grandiflora*
**Approx. height** 90cm (36in)
**Character** Small semi-evergreen shrub with tiny pink or white flowers in summer. Variety '**Gold Spot**' has leaves with an irregular central golden splash.

**Plant** *Acer palmatum*
**(Japanese maple)**
**Approx. height** 200cm (72in)
**Character** The Japanese maples always offer excellent garden value with their attractively shaped foliage, spring and autumn interest. Some hybrids are more like small shrubs and are perfect subjects for growing in containers. **A. p. 'Atropurpureum'** for example, has purple foliage; the **'Dissectum'** form is even more delicate with feathery cut foliage. **A. p. 'D. Crimson Queen'** has a scarlet colouring; **'D. Ornatum'** turns from bronze to red in autumn.

Fig 101   The attractive foliage of Acer palmatum 'Atropurpureum', the ornamental Japanese maple.

*Fig 102*  Arundinaria, *the hardy evergreen genus of bamboo.*

**Plant**  *Berberis* **(Barberry)**
**Approx. height**  30–230cm (12–90in)
**Character**  Both evergreen and deciduous forms of this easy to grow and attractive prickly shrub have fine spring flowers and showy fruits. **B. 'Nana'** is slow growing and mound forming; **B. x antoniana** is an evergreen, also with a rounded habit, deep yellow flowers and blue-black berries. **B. aggregata** has red berries and rewards with a good display of autumn colour.

**Plant**  *Buxus sempervirens* **(Box)**
**Approx. height**  30–40cm (12–16in)
**Character**  Classic slow-growing evergreen with tiny, glossy green leaves for clipping into hedge and topiary shapes. Balls, cones, pyramids and spirals look good in pots in a formal setting; small hedges can be planted in troughs to create visual boundaries. Other forms are more ornamental. **B. s. 'Elegantissima'** makes a natural dome shape and has white markings; **'Gold Tip'** has yellow tips.

**Plant** *Arundinaria japonica*
**Approx. height** 400–500cm (156–192in)
**Character** A hardy bamboo that thrives in semi-shade and which has glossy dark green ribbon-like leaves on its canes. It is a vigorous grower, so is perhaps better restricted within a container. Compost must be kept moist.

**Plant** *Arundinaria murieliae*
**(Elegant Bamboo)**
**Approx. height** 240–300cm (96–120in)
**Character** An attractive bamboo with bright green canes which turn yellow-green.

**Plant** *Camellia japonica*
**'Adolph Audusson'**
**Approx. height** 240cm (96in)
**Character** A compact evergreen camellia with large blood-red blooms. Tolerates part shade.

**Plant** *Caryopteris*
**Approx. height** 100cm (36in)
**Character** Small shrub valued for the soft effect of its grey leaves and blue flower spikes.

**Plant** *Chamaecyparis lawsoniana*
**(Lawson Cypress)**
**Approx. height** 200cm (72in)
**Character** Popular cypress with drooping green foliage.

**Plant** *Choisya ternata*
**(Mexican Orange Blossom)**
**Approx. height** 300cm (120in)
**Character** Prized for its fragrant white flowers in late spring, early summer and its glossy dark green leaves which are also aromatic when bruised. The smaller evergreen *C. t.* **'Sundance'** has light yellow young foliage.

**Plant** *Cordyline australis*
**(Cabbage Palm)**
**Approx. height** 460cm (180in)
**Character** Sword-like evergreen leaves and small creamy summer flowers.

*Fig 103* Choisya ternata *(Mexican Orange Blossom).*

**Plant** *Corylus avellana* **'Contorta'**
**(Corkscrew Hazel)**
**Approx. height** 300cm (120in)
**Character** Small hazel grown for its ornamental spiral stems and showy catkins in late winter.

**Plant** *Cotoneaster*
**Approx. height** 150–500cm (60–120in)
**Character** There is a choice of a large number of types most of which have ornamental berries that are useful for late summer interest. *C. apiculatus* makes arching stems of small round leaves and red fruits, yet the plant does not grow too large. *C. splendens* **'Sabrina'** has small grey-green leaves and orange berries.

**Plant** *Crataegus*
**(Thorn)**
**Approx. height** 450cm (180in)
**Character** The thorns are small ornamental trees with decorative fruits and fine spring blossom. *C. oxyacanthus* **'Paul's Scarlet'** has red double flowers.

**Plant** *Daphne*
**Approx. height** 120cm (48in)
**Character** Choose the smaller hybrids of this shrub, valued for its scented flowers in late winter/early spring; make sure the container is well drained. *D. laureola* is an evergreen with yellow-green flowers; *D. mezereum* thrives in shade and has purple-red flowers and red berries; *D. m.* 'Alba' has white flowers and amber fruits; 'Rosea' has rose pink flowers. *D. odora* forms offer a similar range of colours and are shade-tolerant evergreens.

**Plant** *Euonymus fortunei*
**Approx. height** 45cm (18in)
**Character** Various forms with attractive foliage for winter interest. Choose the smaller types like 'Emerald 'n Gold' which is bushy with gold markings, turning pink in winter; or 'Silver Queen' which has white markings.

**Plant** *Fatsia japonica*
**(False Castor-oil Plant)**
**Approx. height** 200cm (72in)
**Character** A dramatic evergreen with glossy, palmate foliage which prefers part shade.

**Plant** *Hydrangea macrophylla*
**(Lacecap Hydrangea)**
**Approx. height** 150cm (60in)
**Character** The large blooms come in various colours: for example, 'Geoffrey Chadbuned' which is red; 'Blaumeise' which has blue flowers; and 'White Wave' which has white blooms.

**Plant** *Ilex*
**(Holly)**
**Approx. height** 120cm (47in)
**Character** Many forms and colours, with or without spines. Variegated types are useful for different effects. Markings may be yellow, gold, white, cream or silver; stems could be purple, black or green and berries black, red, round or oval.

**Plant** *Juniperus*
**(Juniper)**
**Approx. height** 10–250cm (4–98in)
**Character** A wide choice of varieties whose coloured, needle-like foliage is useful in winter. *J. chinensis* 'Pyramidalis' makes a slow-growing conical blue bush; spreading 'Gold Coast' is golden yellow; 'Embley Park' has drooping branches of grass-green leaves.

**Plant** *Lavandula*
**(Lavender)**
**Approx. height** 45–100cm (18–40in)
**Character** Highly aromatic and sun-loving small shrub which has various forms, all of which are evergreen. *L. angustifolia* 'Alba' has white flowers and narrow grey-green foliage; *L. a.* 'Rosea' has soft pink flowers and compact habit; 'Munstead' is larger but also compact with lavender blue flowers.

*Fig 104* Ilex aquifolium, *useful as a single specimen tree.*

*Fig 105*  Lavandula *is a hardy evergreen with a fine fragrance.*

**Plant**  *Laurus nobilis*
**(Sweet Bay)**
**Approx. height**  150cm (60in)
**Character**  Classic evergreen shrub or standard grown tree for sheltered areas. Glossy green laurel-shaped leaves are aromatic and can be used in cooking. Foliage often clipped into decorative shapes.

**Plant**  *Malus*
**(Flowering Crab)**
**Approx. height**  360cm (144in)
**Character**  Small ornamental tree valued for its stunning spring blossom and interesting autumn fruits. There are many small varieties such as **'Golden Hornet'** with white flowers and plenty of yellow fruit; **'John Downie'**

Fig 106    The crab apple tree is mainly grown for ornamental purposes.

whose large orange-red fruits are edible; and **'Red Jade'** or **'Royal Beauty'** which have red fruits and a weeping habit.

**Plant    *Nandina domestica*
(Heavenly Bamboo)**
**Approx. height**    240cm (96in)
**Character**    A pretty bamboo with delicate pinnate leaves, white flowers and red berries.

**Plant    *Nerium oleander***
**Approx. height**    400cm (160in)
**Character**    Tender shrub with showy fragrant blooms.

**Plant    *Phormium tenax***
**Approx. height**    240cm (96in)
**Character**    A good architectural foliage plant with large sword-like leaves. Hybrids offer colour options: bronze (**'Bronze Baby'**); black (**'Dark Delight'**); red markings (**'Maori Chief'**); apricot (**'Apricot Queen'**), even cream, purple and pink variations.

**Plant    *Phyllostachys aurea*
(Golden Bamboo)**
**Approx. height**    240–300cm (96–120in)
**Character**    Evergreen bamboo with green canes that turn yellow.

**Plant    *Prunus*
(Flowering Cherry)**
**Approx. height**    600cm (240in)
**Character**    Useful small trees producing excellent blossom and foliage colours. ***P. rufa*
'Himalayan Cherry'** also has the added

attraction of peeling red-brown or amber bark; **P. subhirtella 'Autumnalis'**, the autumn cherry and its double or weeping hybrids, bloom at the end of summer.

**Plant   Pyrus**
**(Ornamental Pear)**
**Approx. height**   450cm (180in)
**Character**   A group of small trees useful for special effects: for example, **P. salicifolia 'Pendula'**, the **Weeping Silver Pear**, which has a weeping habit and silver foliage; or **P. communis 'Beech Hill'** which has good autumn colour.

**Plant   Robinia pseudoacacia 'Frisia'**
**(False Acacia)**
**Approx. height**   540cm (216in)
**Character**   A small tree with eye-catching golden-yellow foliage from spring to autumn.

**Plant   Rosmarinus**
**(Rosemary)**
**Approx. height   30–120cm (12–48in)**
**Character**   Shrubby herb which enjoys full sun and looks good in tubs. Needle-like foliage is grey-green and the tiny flowers are blue.

**Plant   Salix**
**(Willow)**
**Approx. height**   300cm (120in)
**Character**   Wide choice of shrub or tree forms, many with attractive foliage and interesting catkins, such as **S. helvetica** or **S. lanata**, the **Woolly Willow**, which is a downy slow grower.

**Plant   Sorbus**
**(Rowan)**
**Approx. height**   540cm (216in)
**Character**   Attractive foliage providing interest in spring, summer and autumn. Many have good berries too: **'Joseph Rock'** (gold); **'Pearly King'** (white/pink); **S. scalaris** (red berries).

**Plant   Taxus baccata**
**(Yew)**
**Approx. height**   240cm (96in)
**Character**   Sombre dark green evergreen conifer which lends itself to being clipped into hedge and topiary shapes. It is a slow grower, so could be grown in a container.

**Plant   Trachycarpus fortunei**
**(Hardy Palm)**
**Approx. height**   200–300cm (72–120in)
**Character**   A good architectural foliage plant with dramatic fan-shaped leaves.

**Plant   Viburnum davidii**
**Approx. height**   75cm (30in)
**Character**   Smallest of the viburnums with glossy leaves and light blue berries.

*Fig 107   Hardy* Viburnum *shrubs have beautiful flowers in winter or spring.*

105

*Fig 108   Interesting Yucca plant on a balcony.*

**Plant   *Yucca***
**Approx. height**   100–200cm (36–72in)
**Character**   Dramatic foliage plant with sword-shaped leaves and creamy-white flower spikes.

## DWARF RHODODENDRONS AND AZALEAS

Dwarf forms of these superb flowering shrubs are perfect for growing in tubs and containers where you can easily maintain an acid soil, since they are lime-haters and do not always do well in the garden. Do not let the compost dry out and combine with heathers and dwarf conifers which enjoy the same conditions.

**Plant   Japanese Azaleas**
**Approx. height**   50–75cm (20–30in)
**Character**   Mostly evergreen or semi-evergreen but prone to late frost, so protect from early morning sun. Range of colours includes **'Blue Danube'** with striking blue blooms; **'Hinomayo'** which makes a mass of pink flowers in late spring; or **'Johanna'** which has bright red flowers against shiny dark green foliage.

**Plant   Deciduous Azaleas**
**Approx. height**   120–150cm (48–60in)
**Character**   Hardy with wonderful flowers and good autumn colour – allow them full sun or light shade. **'Persil'** has white trumpets with an orange-yellow flare; **'Klondyke'** has scented orange flowers and copper-coloured young foliage.

**Plant   Dwarf Rhododendrons**
**Approx. height**   15–90cm (6–35in)
**Character**   A wide choice of sizes, colours and forms including the compact and free-flowering *yakushimanum* hybrids which include bright red against green, **'Dopey'** and low-growing **'Grumpy'** which has pink-tinged yellow trumpets. Also worth considering is tiny **'Chikor'**, a mass of yellow flowers in late spring at a height of 15–20cm (6–8in). Or **'Ramapo'** at 30–40cm (12–16in) which has glaucous green foliage and pale violet flowers.

## CLIMBERS

Climbing plants can be trained up pot supports to create domes, pyramids and cones, or attached to a nearby trellis.

**Plant   *Actinidia chinensis* (Chinese Gooseberry)**
**Character**   Creamy-white flowers and large heart-shaped leaves. Likes plenty of sun and both male and female plants produce the familiar hairy, egg-shaped edible fruits.

**Plant   *Clematis***
**Character**   A large number of types, both evergreen and deciduous, are grown for their spectacular range of flowers. Choose your own favourites from large or small blooms, scented, shade- or sun-lovers.

**Plant   *Clerodendrum thomsoniae***
**Character**   Climber producing mass of red and white flowers.

*Fig 109* Lonicera periclymenum *'Belgica',* a deciduous fragrant climber.

**Plant   *Jasminum nudiflorum***
**(Winter Jasmine)**
**Character**   Delicate green foliage with flowers appearing on the naked branches during the winter.

**Plant   *Lonicera***
**(Honeysuckle)**
**Character**   Various forms of this popular country climber including evergreen and deciduous types, also night- or day-scented flowers.

**Plant   *Parthenocissus quinquefolia***
**(Virginia Creeper)**
**Character**   Good foliage cover – leaves turn a brilliant orange and scarlet in autumn.

**Plant   *Vitis vinifera***
**(Grape Vine)**
**Character**   A useful foliage climber. **'Purpurea'** has claret to deep purple foliage.

# HARDY FERNS

Ferns with their strong feathery fronds make useful foliage contrasts to glossier, larger-leaved plants. A single specimen can look stunning in its own pot or container. Fill with moist compost and keep well watered in a shady position.

**Plant   *Adiantum pedatum***
**(Maidenhair Fern)**
**Approx. height**   25cm (10in)
**Character**   Very hardy fern with dainty foliage.

**Plant   *Asplenium trichomanes***
**(Spleenwort)**
**Approx. height**   7·5–15cm (3–6in)
**Character**   Produces thread-like black stalks with green lobes.

**Plant   *Athyrium filix–femina***
**(Lady Fern)**
**Approx. height**   30cm (24in)
**Character**   Makes tufts of light green fronds.

**Plant   *Blechnum penna–marina***
**Approx. height**   7·5–10cm (3–4in)
**Character**   Young fronds have a coppery colour. This low-growing fern makes a carpet of small, flattened fronds with more erect short, fertile fronds.

**Plant   *Blechnum spicant***
**(Hardy Fern)**
**Approx. height**   25–30cm (10–12in)
**Character**   Useful fern in that it tolerates dry conditions.

**Plant   *Dryopteris dilatata***
**(Broad Buckler Fern)**
**Approx. height**   60–100cm (24–39in)
**Character**   Has broad, divided fronds.

**Plant   *Dryopteris filix-mas***
**(Male Fern)**
**Approx height**   60–100cm (24–39in)

**Character** Reliable fern frequently seen in the wild. Produces a large clump of tough green fronds.

**Plant** *Matteuccia struthiopteris*
**(Ostrich-feather Fern)**
**Approx. height** 100–150cm (36–60in)
**Character** Attractive ornamental fern with large feathery fronds.

**Plant** *Onoclea sensibilis*
**(Sensitive Fern)**
**Approx. height** 50cm (20in)
**Character** Pretty fern that prefers moist conditions.

**Plant** *Osmunda regalis*
**(Royal Fern)**
**Approx. height** 120–200cm (48–78in)
**Character** Large dramatic clump of fronds.

**Plant** *Phyllitis scolopendrium*
**(Hart's-tongue Fern)**
**Approx. height** 50cm (20in)
**Character** A good contrast with flat tongue-like fronds covered in brown spores. An evergreen useful for winter interest.

**Plant** *Polypodium vulgare*
**(Common Polypody)**
**Approx. height** 25–30cm (10–12in)
**Character** Good evergreen that tolerates chalk.

**Plant** *Polystichum aculeatum*
**(Hard Shield Fern)**
**Approx. height** 50–60cm (20–24in)
**Character** An evergreen with strong, dark green fronds.

**Plant** *Polystichum lonchitis*
**(Holly Fern)**
**Approx. height** 30–100cm (12–39in)
**Character** Makes dense tufts of evergreen fronds.

**Plant** *Polystichum setiferum*
**'Plumoso-divisilobum'**
**(Soft Shield Fern)**
**Approx. height** 50cm (20in)
**Character** Has finely divided feathery fronds.

# IVIES

Ivies make excellent evergreen cover in containers, used either as self-clinging climbers over nearby trellis or wired shapes; or to produce ground cover trailing down from hanging baskets or disguising the edge of tubs. There is a spectacular range of different shapes and colours among the *Hedera* genus: silvers and bronzes; dark and light greens; gold; white; cream; and even pink markings.

**Plant** *Hedera canariensis*
**(Canary Island Ivy)**
**Character** Large leaves which turn bronze in winter. Silvery grey and cream-white variegated forms also available.

**Plant** *H. colchica* **'Dentata'**
**(Persian Ivy)**
**Character** Particularly large leaves. Variety **'Sulphur Heart'** has yellow splashes; **'Variegata'** has creamy-yellow margins.

**Plant** *H. helix*
**(Common Ivy)**
**Character** Useful ivy that will grow almost anywhere, even in very shady conditions. There are many variations.

**Plant** *H. h.* **'Cavendishii'**
**Character** Small mottled grey leaves with cream margins.

**Plant** *H. h.* **'Chicago'**
**Character** Small leaves blotched with bronze-purple.

*Fig 110*   Hedera helix *'Goldheart'.*

**Plant   H. h. 'Deltoidea'**
**Character**   Heart-shaped leaves making dense cover that turns bronze in winter.

**Plant   H. h. 'Glacier'**
**Character**   Silver-grey with white margins.

**Plant   H. h 'Goldheart'**
**Character**   Central yellow splash to each leaf.

**Plant   H. h. 'Manda's Crested'**
**Character**   Slow grower with reddish colour in winter.

**Plant   H. h. 'Marginata Elegantissima'**
**Character**   Small grey-green leaves that have pink edges in winter.

**Plant   H. h 'Sagittifolia'**
**Character**   Interesting shaped five-lobed leaves. There is a cream variegated form.

# HOSTAS

Hostas, or plantain lilies, offer an excellent range of plant shapes and colours with their large, pleated foliage, the perfect contrast to feathery or delicate leaves. They produce a dense clump of coloured foliage that is perfect for containers. Soft flower spikes appear in summer, but hostas are grown mainly for their stunning leaves. They look most effective when a single type is allowed to take over the container.

*Fig 111*   *A group of* Hosta *in a nursery.*

**Plant   Hosta albo-marginata**
**Approx. height**   15–20cm (6–8in)
**Character**   Narrow light green leaves with cream margins. Striped flowers are mauve and white.

**Plant   H. 'Elegans'**
**Approx. height**   60cm (24in)
**Character**   Large, round silver-grey leaves with deep indentations.

*Fig 112*   Hosta sieboldiana *'Elegans'.*

**Plant   *H.* fortunei 'Albopicta'**
**Approx. height**   40–50cm (16–20in)
**Character**   Oval yellow-edged leaves which develop dark green margins with age. There is a completely yellow form in spring and summer, **'Aurea'**.

**Plant   *H.* 'Frances Williams'**
**Approx. height**   50–60cm (20–24in)
**Character**   Spectacular blue-grey leaves with beige markings.

**Plant   *H.* 'Halcyon'**
**Approx. height**   30cm (12in)
**Character**   Heart-shaped blue leaves and lilac flowers on purple stems.

**Plant   *H.* 'Honeybells'**
**Approx. height**   30cm (12in)

**Character**   Mauve flowers are scented. Leaves are green.

**Plant   *H. lancifolia***
**Approx. height**   15–18cm (6–7in)
**Character**   Narrow, shiny green leaves.

**Plant   *H.* 'Thomas Hogg'**
**Approx. height**   30cm (12in)
**Character**   Deep green leaves have a wide cream margin. Summer flowers are lilac.

**Plant   *H. undulata***
**Approx. height**   50cm (20in)
**Character**   Wavy green leaves have a central white band.

## HEATHS AND HEATHERS

Producing clumps and carpets of dense colour, heaths and heathers are useful for creating permanent effects according to season. Experiment with winter and autumn flowering types to maintain interest in containers throughout the year. Most prefer a lime-free soil and can be planted up into containers of ericaceous compost in conjunction with rhododendrons and azaleas.

**Plant   *Calluna vulgaris***
**Approx. height**   10–60cm (4–24in)
**Character**   There are many interesting hybrid forms of the evergreen common heather or Ling. A few of the colour variations are set out below.

**Plant   *C. v.* 'Alba Plena'**
**Approx. height**   50cm (20in)
**Character**   Has double white flowers in summer.

**Plant   *C. v.* 'Beoley Gold'**
**Approx. height**   45cm (18in)
**Character**   Late summer white flowers and golden leaves.

**Plant   C. v. 'Blazeaway'**
**Approx. height**   50cm (20in)
**Character**   Mauve flowers in late summer; leaves turn red in winter.

**Plant   C. v. 'Gold Haze'**
**Approx. height**   50cm (20in)
**Character**   White flowers and gold foliage.

**Plant   C. v. 'Orange Queen'**
**Approx. height**   60cm (24in)
**Character**   Pink flowers and gold foliage which turns orange.

**Plant   C. v. 'Robert Chapman'**
**Approx. height**   30–60cm (12–24in)
**Character**   Mauve flowers and golden leaves which turn first orange and then red.

**Plant   C. v. 'Silver Queen'**
**Approx. height**   60cm (24in)
**Character**   Silver-grey leaves and pale mauve flowers.

**Plant   C. v. 'Sister Anne'**
**Approx. height**   10cm (4in)
**Character**   Grey foliage with pink flowers.

**Plant   C. v. 'Tib'**
**Approx. height**   30–60cm (12–14in)
**Character**   Double rosy-red flowers.

**Plant   Erica arborea**
**(Tree Heath)**
**Approx. height**   25cm (10in)
**Character**   Fragrant white flowers in early spring. Hybrids produce purple flowers.

**Plant   E. carnea**
**Approx height**   25cm (10in)
**Character**   Winter flowering, lime-tolerant heather offering a wide choice of colours such as: **'Adrienne Duncan'** with red flowers and dark bronze green foliage; **'Foxhollow'** which has pale pink flowers and yellow foliage with a red tinge in winter; **'Pink Spangles'** which makes a mass of pink flowers in winter; **'Springwood White'** has white winter blooms.

**Plant   E. cinerea**
**(Bell Heather)**
**Approx height**   15–25cm (6–10in)
**Character**   Summer flowering in a wide choice of colours: **'Domino'** is white; **'Golden Drop'** has pink flowers with golden foliage which turns rusty-red in winter; **'P.S. Patrick'** has purple flowers.

**Plant   E. mediterranea**
**Approx. height**   200cm (72in)
**Character**   Very small with rose red spring flowers. Lime-tolerant. Hybrids include a grey and green foliage and white flowers.

*Fig 113*   Calluna vulgaris.

**Plant**   *E. vagans*
**(Cornish Heath)**
**Approx. height**   120cm (48in)
**Character**   Makes long sprays of flowers from summer through to autumn. There are many varieties with pink, white and cerise flowers and yellow foliage.

**Plant**   *E. x williamsii* **'P.D. Williams'**
**Character**   Rose pink flowers in summer through to autumn. Yellow-tipped leaves turn bronze by winter.

# CONIFERS

Dwarf and slow-growing conifers are perfect for containers and window-boxes. Compact in size and offering an interesting range of shapes and colours, they can be an important element of your backbone planting scheme. Many species will naturally grow into domes, pyramids and spires in a choice of blue, green, gold and silver foliage colours. Grow them alone; create a mini-woodland by combining with shrubs and heathers to get a range of heights; or use them architecturally in order to devise interesting contrasts.

**Plant**   *Abies concolor*
**'Compacta'**
**Approx. height**   60–90cm (24–35in)
**Character**   A dwarf fir with an irregular rounded habit and silver-blue leaves.

**Plant**   *A. koreana*
**Approx. height**   150–200cm (60–78in)
**Character**   Dark green upper leaves are silvery-white beneath with eye-catching blue cylindrical cones.

**Plant**   *A. nordmanniana*
**'Golden Spreader'**
**Approx. height**   20–30cm (8–12in)
**Character**   A neat bush of golden-yellow needles.

**Plant**   *Cedrus libani* **'Sargentii'**
**Approx. height**   60–90cm (24–35in)
**Character**   Weeping habit produces a dense spread of green.

**Plant**   *Chamaecyparis lawsoniana*
**'Aurea Densa'**
**Approx. height**   30–50cm (12–20in)
**Character**   Makes a dense dome of golden yellow foliage.

**Plant**   *C. l.* **'Ellwood's Pillar'**
**Approx. height**   75–100cm (30–39in)
**Character**   Produces a narrow compact pillar of feathery blue-grey.

**Plant**   *C. l.* **'Gnome'**
**Approx. height**   20–30cm (8–12in)
**Character**   A tiny, deep green specimen.

**Plant**   *C. l.* **'Little Spire'**
**Approx. height**   150–200cm (60–78in)
**Character**   Grows slowly into a green column which eventually produces attractive red 'flowers' in spring.

**Plant**   *C. l.* **'Nana Albospica'**
**Approx. height**   75cm (30in)
**Character**   White foliage looks almost like snow in summer.

**Plant**   *C. l.* **'Pygmy'**
**Approx. height**   30cm (12in)
**Character**   Makes a tiny mound of grey-green leaves.

**Plant**   *C. pisifera* **'Gold Spangle'**
**(Sawara Cypress)**
**Approx. height**   90cm (35in)
**Character**   Rounded habit and bright gold foliage for good winter colour.

**Plant**   *C. p.* **'Plumosa Compressa'**
**Approx. height**   20–30cm (8–12in)
**Character**   Makes a tiny, compact mound of pale yellow foliage.

**Plant**   *C. p.* **'Plumosa Purple Dome'**
**Approx. height**   50–60cm (20–24in)
**Character**   Feathery grey foliage has a purple tint in winter.

**Plant**   *C. thyoides* **'Rubicon'**
**Approx. height**   60cm (24in)
**Character**   Compact bronze green foliage turns a rich red in winter.

**Plant**   *Cryptomeria japonica* **'Compressa'**
**Approx. height**   30–40cm (12–16in)
**Character**   Small and compact forming a flat-topped globe of green foliage tinted a reddish-purple in winter.

**Plant**   *C. j.* **'Vilmoriniana'**
**Approx. height**   30–40cm (12–16in)
**Character**   Grows slowly to produce a neat globe of fresh green.

**Plant**   *Microbiota decussata*
**Approx. height**   20–30cm (8–12in)
**Character**   Low-growing spread of lacy but dense green foliage which turns bronze in winter.

**Plant**   *Picea abies* **'Little Gem'**
**Approx. height**   20–30cm (8–12in)
**Character**   Makes a dense ball of green with attractive new shoots in spring.

**Plant**   *P. glauca* **'Aurina'**
**Approx. height**   40cm (16in)
**Character**   This fresh green, compact pyramid is the ideal miniature for sink and container gardens.

**Plant**   *P. mariana* **'Nana'**
**Approx. height**   15–20cm (6–8in)
**Character**   Slow-growing blue ball perfect for troughs and sinks.

**Plant**   *Pinus mugo* **'Humpy'**
**Approx. height**   30–40cm (12–16in)

*Fig 114*   Pinus mugo.

**Character**   Makes a dense round bush of short green needles and prominent winter buds.

**Plant**   *P. m.* **'Wintergold'**
**Approx. height**   40–50cm (16–20in)
**Character**   Bright golden form through the winter which then turns light green during the summer.

**Plant**   *P. primula* **'Dwarf Blue'**
**Approx. height**   40–50cm (16–20in)
**Character**   Slow-growing spreader which produces clusters of attractive blue and white needles.

**Plant**   *P. strobus* **'Reinshaus'**
**Approx. height**   60cm (24in)
**Character**   Small, compact bush which needs good drainage. Makes a dense display of glaucous needles.

**Plant** *P. sylvestris* **'Hibernica'**
**Approx. height** 50–60cm (20–24in)
**Character** Makes a compact round bush of grey-blue needles and prominent winter buds.

**Plant** *Taxus baccata* **'Corley's Coppertip'**
**Approx. height** 30–40cm (12–16in)
**Character** Copper-coloured leaves turn to green with whitish markings. Semi-prostrate form.

**Plant** *T. b.* **'Summergold'**
**Approx. height** 40–50cm (16–20in)
**Character** Bright golden yellow foliage in summer.

**Plant** *Thuja occidentalis* **'Danica'**
**Approx. height** 30–45cm (12–18in)
**Character** Compact globe of dark green turns bronze in winter.

**Plant** *T. orientalis* **'Golden Ball'**
**Approx. height** 40–50cm (16–20in)
**Character** Dome-shaped bush of bright yellow turns green and later bronze.

**Plant** *T. plicata* **'Rogersii'**
**Approx. height** 30–45cm (12–18in)
**Character** Good for winter colour, turning from green to golden bronze.

**Plant** *Tsuga canadensis* **'Jeddeloh'**
**Approx. height** 30–40cm (12–16in)
**Character** Graceful, light green foliage and semi-prostrate habit.

# SPRING INTEREST

Plants grown in tubs and containers come into their own in spring when there may be little else of interest showing in the garden. Large, permanent containers can be planted up with bulbs and spring flowers for a seasonal display; or smaller containers can be kept under wraps in a sheltered place to force a few early blooms and introduce on to the terrace, patio or around the garden for a little extra early spring cheer. Your permanent planting may provide spring blossom (*see* Trees and Shrubs, p 61), but it is mainly to the bulbs we turn for the welcoming sight and scent of fresh spring flowers. When bulbs are past their best, they should be removed ready for summer planting; plant them out in a spare bed until the leaves have died back when they can be lifted and cleaned, and stored in a cool dry place to be used in the garden next season, but buy fresh bulbs for your pots. There are many shorter or dwarf forms which are ideally suited to smaller containers and are worth looking out for if you want to create a more delicate display.

**Plant** *Clivia miniata* **(Kaffir Lily)**
**Approx. height** 50cm (18in)
**Character** Very elegant with bold, tongue-like leaves and large clusters of orange, trumpet-shaped blooms.

**Plant** *Chionodoxa* **(Glory of the Snow)**
**Approx. height** 7·5–10cm (3–4in)
**Character** Grown for its pretty blue star-shaped flowers, this hardy perennial flowers early in the spring.

**Plant** *Crocus*
**Approx. height** 5–13cm (2–5in)
**Character** Plant in massed groups to get the best effect from their low carpet of bright, waxy colour. They are good for planting under taller spring flowers and offer a choice of large or small, open or closed blooms, and a range of colours from purples, golds, pinks and whites to striped patterns.

**Plant** *Cyclamineus narcissi*
**Approx. height** 20–30cm (8–12in)
**Character** Various colour types and a dwarf habit that makes them excellent for tubs.

**Plant** *Erythronium*
**Approx. height** 30cm (12in)
**Character** There are various types with their lovely spotted foliage and beautiful, nodding blooms. Useful since they will tolerate light shade. The **Trout Lily**, *E. californicum* has cream flowers; **Dog's-tooth Violet**, *E. denscanis*, has mauve to pink flowers.

**Plant** *Freesia refracta*
**Approx. height** 50cm (18in)
**Character** Sweet scented, delicate flowers in a blend of clear, complementary colours.

**Plant** *Galanthus*
**(Snowdrop)**
**Approx. height** 10–25cm (4–10in)
**Character** These are usually the first flowers to be seen, pushing their white bells through snow or chilly soil as early as the beginning of the year. Look out for varieties with larger flowers, frills or interesting green markings.

**Plant** **Garden Hyacinth**
**Approx. height** 30–38cm (12–15in)
**Character** Best for tubs and containers are the *Multiflora* types which produce several spikes of white, blue or pink. **'Pink Pearl'** and **'Anna Marie'** are pink; **'Carnegie'** is white; **'City of Harlem'** is yellow; the early **'Ostara'** and **'Delft Blue'** have blue spikes.

**Plant** *Muscari* **(Grape Hyacinth)**
**Approx. height** 15–20cm (6–8in)
**Character** Miniature spikes of deep, dark blue and delicate scent. Can look superb beneath taller plants or fronting a window-box display.

**Plant** **Narcissi** and **Daffodil**
**Approx. height** 38–61cm (12–24in)
**Character** A wide range of colours and styles is available, including double flowers, frills and special markings if you want to create a display of particular interest: eg **N. 'Salome'** which has a pink crown; **N. 'Marie Jose'**, a butterfly type with yellow star-shaped markings; and **N. 'Petit Four'** which is a double flowered type with peach coloured frilly centres.

**Plant** *Narcissus asturiensis*
**Approx. height** 8–10cm (3–4in)
**Character** Miniature early flowering form with a wide range of flower types including tiny trumpet daffodils.

**Plant** *N. jonquilla*
**Approx. height** 15–25cm (6–10in)
**Character** Sweet scented variety that does well in tubs.

**Plant** *N. triandrus*
**Approx. height** 15–40cm (6–16in)
**Character** A shorter growing, multi-headed variety with interesting bloom shapes.

*Fig 115   A colourful patio display of* Polyanthus.

**Plant**  *Polyanthus*
**Approx. height**   18cm (7in)
**Character**   Dense display of bright flowers of many colours amongst thick green leaves.

**Plant**  *Primula*
**Approx. height**   18cm (7in)
**Character**   The semi-miniature, early flowering primroses are prettiest for pots.

**Plant**  *Scilla*
**(Woodland Bluebells)**
**Approx. height**   10cm (4in)
**Character**   Delicate nodding bells of blue, white and pink.

**Plant**  **Tulip**
**Approx. height**   30–66cm (12–26in)
**Character**   Valuable for adding exactly the colour you want later in the season, since tulips are available in an extraordinary range of shades and shapes from single and double early blooms to special hybrids and late-blooming types, exotic parrot tulips, elegant lily flowered varieties, blacks, reds, whites, blues, yellows – even stripes and frills.

**Plant**  *Tulipa greigii*
**Approx. height**   15–30cm (6–12in)
**Character**   A dwarf type good for window-boxes and tubs and available in a range of colours: **'Princess Charmante'** is scented; **'Red Riding Hood'** is red with stripes.

**Plant**  *Cheiranthus cheiri*
**(Wallflower)**
**Approx. height**   38–46cm (15–18in)
**Character**   Useful rich early colours – plant into tubs when bushy before winter. Look out for the new compact forms in pastel colours.

## SUMMER INTEREST

You will want your containers to look their best right through the summer months and it is possible to plan for certain high points throughout the season with perennials such as roses and dianthus. To maintain the display and keep the interest up right through, bright flowered annuals provide the chance to create spectacular effects and to experiment with different colour combinations from year to year. You should take care to get your young plants in early so that they have time to spread and bloom – some people prefer to plant up complete containers and put them on display only when ready. Remove and replace plants when they are past their best.

**Plant**  *Alyssum*
**Approx. height**   8–10cm (3–4in)
**Character**   Makes a close-growing carpet of white or gold, useful for edging or softening the rim of containers. White alyssum is handy for positioning with stronger deeper colours that need lightening.

**Plant**  *Antirrhinum*
**Approx. height**   20–30cm (8–12in)
**Character**   Easy to grow in a wide range of colours – dwarf forms like **'Little Gem'** are best for pots.

**Plant**  **African Marigold**
**Approx. height**   25–60cm (10–24in)
**Character**   Large golden blooms are a real eye-catcher and plants come in a choice of sizes from tall standing at 60cm (24in), middling at 46–60cm (18–24in) and low growing at 25–30cm (10–14in).

**Plant**  *Begonia semperflorens*
**Approx. height**   25–50cm (9–18in)
**Character**   Valued for their combination of glossy, green leaves and waxy flowers in shades of red, pink and white.

**Plant**  *Calceolaria*
**Approx. height**   25cm (10in)
**Character**   Makes a mass of golden bubbles against green foliage.

Fig 116   An excellent collection of Coleus.

**Plant   *Campanula fragilis* (Creeper) (Basket Campanula)**
**Character**   Trailing stems of large, pale blue flowers can look superb in pots and hanging baskets. Other forms have purple or dark blue flowers.

**Plant   *Cineraria maritima***
**Approx. height**   23–50cm (9–12in)
**Character**   Prized for its crisped silver foliage, a good highlight and companion to other plants. Likes a sunny situation.

**Plant   *Coleus blumei***
**Approx. height**   50cm (18in)
**Character**   Strongly marked, coloured foliage plants in shades of dark red, yellow, green, cream and black.

**Plant   *Dianthus***
**Approx. height**   10–45cm (4–18in)
**Character**   Pretty pinks and carnations make

Fig 117   French marigold.

a sweet scented addition to old-fashioned tubs and pots in shades of pink, white and red.

**Plant  French Marigold**
**Approx. height**  30cm (12in)
**Character**  Splendid range of free-flowering golden blooms against feathery green foliage.

**Plant  *Fuchsia***
**Approx. height**  60cm (24in)
**Character**  Many hybrid forms produce both large and small exotic dangling blooms in various combinations of purples, pinks and whites. Fuchsias are excellent plants for use in hanging baskets and tubs.

**Plant  *Geranium***
**Approx. height**  30–38cm (12–15in)
**Character**  Always popular plants for pots with their attractive foliage and red, pink and white flowers. Choose varieties specially recommended for growing in pots and tubs: the ivy-leaved types are good for hanging baskets; cascading and trailing types are useful for balconies and hanging baskets over which they can trail 46cm (18in). Some have scented leaves and are ideally positioned close at hand on a patio or in a scented garden.

**Plant  *Impatiens* (Busy Lizzie)**
**Approx. height**  25cm (10in)
**Character**  Will tolerate cool shade producing the familiar profusion of red, pink, white or striped flowers.

**Plant  *Lobelia***
**Approx. height**  30cm (12in)
**Character**  The cascade types are perfect for hanging baskets making a ball of pink or purple flowers. Combines well with other plants or grow several shades in the one container.

**Plant  *Lysimachia nummularia***
**(Creeping Jenny)**
**Approx. height**  (Creeper)
**Character**  Tiny green leaves and yellow flowers useful for window-boxes and hanging baskets providing the soil is kept moist.

**Plant  *Mimulus***
**(Monkey flower)**
**Approx. height**  15–30cm (6–12in)
**Character**  Good strong colour for window-boxes and hanging baskets. The flowers are strong burgundy and gold, some of them interestingly blotched.

**Plant  *Paludosum***
**(Miniature Marguerite)**
**Approx. height**  23–30cm (9–12in)
**Character**  Feathery green foliage studded with daisies.

**Plant  Pansy**
**Approx. height**  15–20cm (6–8in)
**Character**  A great many different colours and markings for creating special combinations.

**Plant  *Petunia***
**Approx. height**  30cm (12in)
**Character**  The compact forms are good for hanging baskets and produce a mass of frilled and sometimes striped trumpets of purple, pink, blue, red or yellow.

**Plant  Pot Marigold**
**Approx. height**  30–38cm (12–15in)
**Character**  Reliable display of golden flowers and green foliage.

**Plant  *Salvia***
**Approx. height**  25–30cm (10–12in)
**Character**  Long lasting, with bright red spikes above marked green fleshy foliage.

**Plant  *Sedum sieboldii variegatum***
**Approx. height**  (Creeper)
**Character**  Pretty cream and blue or green foliage.

*Fig 118 (opposite)  Plant petunias in many different colours for a fine display in the summer.*

**Plant** *Tagetes*
**Approx. height**   23cm (9in)
**Character**   Many varieties forming mounds of tiny yellow, gold or bronze flowers among dense, bright green feathery foliage.

**Plant** *Tropaeolum majus*
**(Nasturtium)**
**Approx. height**   23cm (9in)
**Character**   Attractive bright green leaves and gaily coloured yellow and orange flowers that flourish in poor soil and hot, dry conditions. A height of 23cm (9in) on the shorter forms.

**Plant** *Verbena*
**Approx. height**   15–30cm (6–12in)
**Character**   Pointed leaves and flowers ranging from purple to scarlet or blue.

## ROSES

An attractive permanent feature within a romantic or old-fashioned patio scheme, the smaller forms of the compact bush roses can do well in containers. Keep watered and mulch well, feeding generously during the flowering season. There are various basic types to choose from.

**Plant   Large Flowered Bush Rose**
**(Hybrid Tea)**
**Approx. height**   Low growing types reach 75cm (30in)
**Character**   Wide choice of colours: **'Abbeyfield'** has a compact habit and is a soft red; small bushy **'Pot o'Gold'** has scented yellow-gold flowers.

**Plant   Cluster Flowered Bush Roses**
**(Floribundas)**
**Approx. height**   Smaller types to 45cm (18in)
**Character**   Excellent colours and plenty of compact forms – often called patio roses: **'Elegant Pearl'** is dense, compact and long flowering with creamy white flowers; **'Gentle**

**Touch'** produces pink flowers in clusters; **'Robin Redbreast'** is dark red with a yellow or white eye.

**Plant   Ramblers** and **Climbers**
**Approx. height**   180cm (72in)
**Character**   Grow over a frame or nearby trellis. **'Swany'** has double white blooms and thrives in shade; **'Bobbie James'** produces small, fragrant cream flowers; **'Paul's Scarlet Climber'** is a semi-double brilliant red form.

**Plant   Miniature Roses**
**Approx. height**   30cm (12in)
**Character**   Pretty for small containers with delicate foliage and pink, white or red flowers.

## AUTUMN INTEREST

Avoid that sad, end-of-season look by planning a display of autumn flowering bulbs and plants to inject extra colour and interest into your scheme, many of which will continue through into winter. Remember to remove summer flowering plants when they start to look past their best. *See* also 'Trees and Shrubs' on page 61 for valuable autumn interest.

**Plant** *Begonia x tuberhybrida*
**(Tuberous Begonia)**
**Approx. height**   30cm (12in)
**Character**   Grand and colourful with their bright blossoms: the Pendula types are best for hanging baskets; choose **'Multiflora Maxima'** for tubs.

**Plant** *Bergenia*
**(Elephant's Ears)**
**Approx. height**   30cm (12in)
**Character**   Mainly grown for its giant fleshy leaves but produces pretty white, pink or red flowers.

**Plant   Dwarf Chrysanthemum**
**Approx. height**   30–38cm (12–15in)

**Character** Pom pom types in rich autumn shades of red and gold.

**Plant** *Colchicum autumnale*
**Approx. height** 10–15cm (4–6in)
**Character** There are various free-flowering varieties producing mauve or white star-shaped flowers.

**Plant** *Crinum x powellii*
**Approx. height** 60–90cm (24–36in)
**Character** A tender plant for sheltered spots with amaryllis-like, huge, scented trumpets of pink or white.

**Plant** *Cyclamen*
**Approx. height** 8cm (3in)
**Character** There are various winter and autumn flowering types, the cluster of butterfly-like blooms in white or pink making an exotic splash of shape and colour. Some types are scented.

**Plant** *Galtonia candicans*
**Approx. height** 60–76cm (24–30in)
**Character** Produces spikes of white bell-like flowers.

**Plant** *Iris histrioides*
**Approx. height** 5cm (2in)
**Character** Blue blooms in late autumn to early winter.

**Plant** *Iris danfordiae*
**Approx. height** 5cm (2in)
**Character** Has yellow flowers.

**Plant** *Nerine bowdenii*
**Approx. height** 45cm (18in)
**Character** Has lovely pink, lily-like flowers.

**Plant** *Ranunculus*
**Approx. height** 30cm (12in)
**Character** A wide variety of pinks, yellows and reds with a choice of double or semi-double forms.

**Plant** *Solanum capsicastrum* (**Winter Cherry**)
**Approx. height** 23–38cm (9–15in)
**Character** A good splash of colour for window-boxes and small pots, the plants look like miniature green bushes studded with bright orange 'cherries'.

**Plant** *Sternbergia lutea*
**Approx. height** 15cm (6in)
**Character** Has flowers like a yellow crocus.

**Plant** *Vallota speciosa* (**Scarborough Lily**)
**Approx. height** 60cm (24in)
**Character** A tender but spectacular plant for sheltered areas with its brilliant red trumpet flowers.

**Plant** *Zephyranthes candida*
**Approx. height** 15–30cm (6–12in)
**Character** A tender plant with white starry flowers and grass-like leaves.

# EDIBLES

Many fruits and vegetables adapt well to being container grown, particularly compact and tender varieties which can be supplied with tubs of the correct compost and positioned to catch exactly the right amount of sun or shade. For those with only small gardens, it may be the only way to taste the delights of your own produce. Plants will require conscientious watering and feeding during the growing season.

**Vegetable** **Aubergine**
**Approx. height** 90cm (36in)
**Character** **'Slim Jim'** is a decorative plant with purple leaves and small fruits 7cm (3in) long.

**Vegetable** **Corn Salad**
**Approx. height** 10cm (4in)
**Character** Sometimes known as **Lamb's**

Fig 119  *It is quite possible to grow cucumbers in pots on the patio.*

**Lettuce**, this is a tasty salad plant that can be grown almost all year round. The narrow leaves are eaten young.

**Vegetable   Mini Cucumbers**
**Approx. height**   12–18cm (5–7in)
**Character**   Can grow indoors or on a sheltered patio in 25cm (10in) pots. **'Petita'** produces cucumbers 20cm (8in) long.

**Vegetable   Dwarf French Bean**
**Approx. height**   30cm (12in)
**Character**   **'Royal Burgundy'** has attractive purple flowers and purple pods and is decorative as well as useful.

**Vegetable   Lettuce**
**Approx. height**   6–9cm (2–4in)
**Character**   Grow the more decorative varieties like **'Novita'** which makes an ornamental ball of curved leaves.

**Vegetable   Peas**
**Approx. height**   45cm (18in)
**Character**   A dwarf, early variety like **'Hurst Beagle'** which has an excellent flavour, could quite easily be grown in a container.

**Vegetable   Sweet Pepper**
**Approx. height**   30–40cm (12–16in)
**Character**   Plants with a dwarf habit like *Capsicum* **'Redskin F'** are ideal for tubs and produce fruits around a central stem in August or September.

**Vegetable   Radish**
**Approx. height**   45cm (18in)
**Character**   A tasty treat from the minimum of space: **'Cherry Bell'** is a fast grower making round, red radishes; **'China Rose'** is a winter radish, long and pink.

Fig 120    *Home-grown tomatoes are a delicious addition to your summer salads.*

## Vegetable    Tomatoes

**Approx. height**    45cm (18in)

**Character**    Some varieties are perfect for pots or even the specially designed strawberry containers. Choose a self-supporting type with fruits clustered round a central stem for growing in tubs. Alternatively, one of the tiny cherry tomato types like the sweet tasting **'Small Fry'** or **'Gardener's Delight'** is ideal.

## FRUITS

Strawberries may be the obvious choice for fruit on the patio but container growing is the perfect opportunity to grow more tender fruit trees and bushes in pots as standards or in dwarf pyramids, to be moved into more sheltered conditions at the end of summer. Select small, compact varieties with good yields for best results.

**Fruit Apricot**
**Character** 'Hemskirk' has conical fruits and a heavy yield.

**Fruit Berries**
**Character** Blackberry **'Oregon Thornless'** has no prickles and a heavy yield; also consider some of the interesting hybrid berries now available, like the hardy boysenberry, long-fruited loganberry or mild flavoured tayberry.

**Fruit Currants**
**Character** Blackcurrant **'Baldwin'** makes a compact, high-yielding plant.

**Fruit Gooseberry**
**Character** 'Golden Drop' is compact with a good flavour.

**Fruit Nectarine**
**Character** 'Humboldt' has attractive blossom and fruits and makes a decorative addition to the patio.

**Fruit Orange**
**Character** Grow *Citrus sinensis* as a standard in the greenhouse or conservatory and bring outside in summer.

**Fruit Peach**
**Character** 'Duke of York' has a good flavour.

**Fruit Pear**
**Character** 'Durondeau' is self-fertile and has compact growth.

**Fruit Strawberry**
**Character** Grow in special tubs or pots that allow the plants to fruit from the sides. A large tub requires 0.2sq m (2.5sq ft) of space and holds 30–50 plants depending on height. One of the best varieties for growing in tubs is **'Aromel'** which has a good flavour and a long cropping season well into autumn.

# HERBS

Herbs seem perfectly suited to pots of all sizes whether it be a tiny pot on a shelf or table, or a large tub standing on the patio. You can put together a collection of your own favourites to use in cooking; or simply grow herbs for the decorative effect of the scented flowers and foliage.

**Herb Bush Basil**
**Approx. height** 25cm (10in)
**Character** *Ocimum minimum* is the best choice for pots with its small, compact foliage.

**Herb Chives**
**Approx. height** 23cm (9in)
**Character** Their spiky grass-like foliage and pink pom pom flowers make a good contrast to other plants.

**Herb Garlic Chives**
**Approx. height** 30cm (12in)
**Character** Chives with a mild garlic onion flavour and white flowers.

**Herb Marjoram**
**Approx. height** 25–30cm (10–12in)
**Character** An attractive bush of small leaves and soft pink flowers.

**Herb Mint**
**Approx. height** 15cm (6in)
**Character** Many varieties with different scents and flavours and including variegated foliage types. Container growing helps to limit vigorous growth which normally makes mints unsuitable in the garden.

**Herb Parsley**
**Approx. height** 15–30cm (6–12in)
**Character** 'Curlina' is a tightly curled compact form, dark green and very attractive – ideal for pots.

*Fig 121    Grey sage with yellow summer flowers.*

**Herb   Rosemary**
**Approx. height**   60cm–120cm (24–48in)
**Character**   An excellent shrubby bush of spiky, strongly aromatic foliage and soft blue flowers.

**Herb   Sage**
**Approx. height**   30cm (12in)
**Character**   Soft grey or purple foliage plant although it does produce attractive flowers in summer.

*Fig 122    A collection of herbs for the kitchen window sill.*

**Herb   Savory**
**Approx. height**   30–45cm (12–18in)
**Character**   Summer and winter varieties make an attractive small-leaved plant. A useful pot herb.

**Herb   Tarragon**
**Approx. height**   100cm (36in)
**Character**   French tarragon has the better flavour. Narrow, flat green leaves make an attractive plant.

**Herb   Thyme**
**Approx. height**   23–30cm (9–12in)
**Character**   Many varieties offer variegated and coloured foliage forms, and some have flowers of lilac, pink, red or white. There are also creeping thymes which make excellent plants for softening the edges of pots.

# Index

**Note**   Page numbers of illustrations are indicated in italic type.